FROGS AND SCORPIONS

FROGS AND SCORPIONS

Linden Fielding

Frogs and Scorpions

Copyright © 2023 by Linden Fielding. All rights reserved.

No part of this publication may be reproduced, stored in a retrieval system or transmitted in any way by any means, electronic, mechanical, photocopy, recording or otherwise without the prior permission of the author except as provided by USA copyright law.

This novel is a work of fiction. Names, descriptions, entities, and incidents included in the story are products of the author's imagination. Any resemblance to actual persons, events, and entities is entirely coincidental.

The opinions expressed by the author are not necessarily those of URLink Print and Media.

1603 Capitol Ave., Suite 310 Cheyenne, Wyoming USA 82001
1-888-980-6523 | admin@urlinkpublishing.com

URLink Print and Media is committed to excellence in the publishing industry.

Book design copyright © 2023 by URLink Print and Media. All rights reserved.

Published in the United States of America

Library of Congress Control Number: 2023914723
ISBN 978-1-68486-485-0 (Paperback)
ISBN 978-1-68486-492-8 (Digital)

03.08.23

PREFACE

Capitalists, socialists, communists, and dictatorships are the dramatically different ideologies and governments around the world. But the universal need for food, shelter, and infrastructure are in every country of the world. Saudi Arabia is known for its oil exports to countries all around the globe. To a lesser extent, Saudi Arabia also exports cement powder. This story is about Saudi Cement Company, an exporter of cement powder, and Dome Technology, an American company that was contracted to build a cement export terminal in Saudi Arabia.

This is a true story of how this common need and agreement was overshadowed by the vastly different social and cultural norms. The resulting conflict threatened to destroy one or both companies.

In today's politically correct environment, some may cringe at this blatant illustration of a business conflict between two profoundly different cultures. When it comes to commerce, communication, and travel, we are in one world where it is just as easy to call or communicate with someone across an ocean as it is across town or across the street.

Chapter 1

"Two million dollars!" shouted the Arab. "You took two million dollars from us!" Veins stood out on his neck and forehead as he shouted. His eyes were bloodshot and buggy. He stood up from his chair and shook his fist. With every word, a spray of spit added to the verbal barrage levied at the three Americans across the table—three Americans against ten from the Saudi Arabian company.

The Arab was furious he was in this situation at this point. His pride was badly battered. There would have been some honor in a physical wound with a knife or bullet. But to him, this was treachery of the highest order. They had been outmaneuvered in their home country, their hometown. They had grown smug, feeling they held all the cards and had all the control. That smugness gave them a blind spot, and it had been exploited.

The situation had become desperate, and desperate measures were taken to preserve the Americans in the room and the company they represented. This was the climax, the last assault, that would ultimately determine who returned home successful and who would return demoralized. Life for those sitting on both sides of the table would be different after today.

The battleground was not a muddy, pockmarked field on a dreary battlefield but a posh London office where the two sides had met before. The Saudi's were not shy about flaunting their wealth. It was acceptable middle ground for both sides.

The Americans sat silent. They had expected the tirade and stoically sat, allowing the storm to rage.

A major casualty of the conflict was already apparent, Mr. Al-Hossari, the boorish, grizzled, project manager of the Saudi company had been left at home, out of the battle. Much of the conflict and focus of this summit had been precipitated by his inflammatory words, arrogance, and misjudgments.

Three Years Earlier

The project got underway three years earlier when the Saudi company sought bids to build a cement export facility at the Port of Dammam in Saudi Arabia. They insisted the general contractor be an American company and provide the latest in technology. The unspoken reason was they wanted the bragging rights that came with employing an American company. Neither company was large on the global stage, but both companies were familiar with international business.

"I bring you a request to bid on a cement export terminal to be built in Dammam, Saudi Arabia," explained Harry James. Harry had been born in Iraq. He emigrated and settled in Canada in the 1980s, when permission for such a move was easy to obtain. Harry was a college professor but found his knowledge and contacts in the Middle East were far more valuable than teaching. He helped Canadian and American companies do business in the Middle East by greasing the wheels between the two vastly different cultures and business norms.

Besides Harry, there were only two companies in the meeting that day in Pennsylvania: the one I represented, which would build the large reinforced concrete domes to store several shiploads of cement powder, and a mechanical company, Fuller, who would supply and install much of the critical machinery necessary to move the product to a waiting ship.

"We are interested," I said after hearing specifics of the project. "I'll gather information and should have you a preliminary bid by this time next week."

I had been at Dome Technology for seven years as the general manager. As such, I was usually involved in sales of the larger projects. The owner and chairman of the board was an imaginative and talented inventor but lacking in business and financial aptitude. I was hired to improve the financial footing and grow the company. It didn't take long after being hired to learn that the company was broke and operating on fumes.

It took several years, but with a revised advertising program, sales effort, and financial policy, the company was on solid footing and growing over twenty percent a year.

"Good," said Harry. "And there is one more thing. Linden, your company needs to be the general contractor on this job."

"That is not a good idea," I immediately protested. "Our company has never been the general contractor on a job like this. It would make more sense for Fuller to be the general contractor. They are a much larger company and have done business in Saudi Arabia before."

"We've already considered it," injected the Fuller representative. "But it's against our company policy."

"The Saudi company has asked that an American company be the general contractor," argued Harry. "They have several reasons for requiring this. If you want a shot at landing this project, your company needs to step up."

"To build the storage buildings is no problem, even in Saudi Arabia. But, taking on the position of general contractor is a whole different ballgame. I can't give you an answer until I discuss it with the chairman of the board. I can tell you now, I'm not in favor of it. It pushes us too far beyond our experience."

A project like this one may have ten subcontractors. Two or three will make up seventy-five percent of the work. However, all the payments, inspections, warranties on the work, workmanship, permits, and approvals by the local officials become the responsibility of the general contractor, so the owner has only one company to deal with for the project. A management fee, usually a percentage of the total project, is added to compensate the general contractor.

Chapter 2

"I don't like it, Barry," I said the day I returned and met with the majority stockholder and chairman of the board. "It puts us beyond anything we've done before and certainly puts me beyond my experience and out of my comfort zone."

Barry stroked his chin. We had done a project in the UAE, the United Arab Emirates, before and other parts of Asia and Europe, but not as the general contractor. "How much do you think the whole project will be?" he asked slowly.

"About twenty million," I replied. This was over ten times our usual jobs.

His eyes grew wide. His face flushed. A smile instantly appeared. I could almost see dollar signs appear in his eyes. "Twenty million," he muttered.

"Barry, I'm against it," I insisted. I could see I was losing the argument and needed to put all the cards on the table. "The risk is too great. We have no experience with a job this complicated. There are so many unknowns. And it's in Saudi Arabia. Remember Mel Brown's Company just down the street? They went bankrupt trying to do business there. It's a different business climate. We could easily be tripped up by customs or requirements we're not even aware of. We've always been the subcontractor on jobs like this. The general contractor provides a cushion between the foreign company and us. With this job, we'll be the intermediary between the Saudis and the

I had been at Dome Technology for seven years as the general manager. As such, I was usually involved in sales of the larger projects. The owner and chairman of the board was an imaginative and talented inventor but lacking in business and financial aptitude. I was hired to improve the financial footing and grow the company. It didn't take long after being hired to learn that the company was broke and operating on fumes.

It took several years, but with a revised advertising program, sales effort, and financial policy, the company was on solid footing and growing over twenty percent a year.

"Good," said Harry. "And there is one more thing. Linden, your company needs to be the general contractor on this job."

"That is not a good idea," I immediately protested. "Our company has never been the general contractor on a job like this. It would make more sense for Fuller to be the general contractor. They are a much larger company and have done business in Saudi Arabia before."

"We've already considered it," injected the Fuller representative. "But it's against our company policy."

"The Saudi company has asked that an American company be the general contractor," argued Harry. "They have several reasons for requiring this. If you want a shot at landing this project, your company needs to step up."

"To build the storage buildings is no problem, even in Saudi Arabia. But, taking to take on the position of general contractor is a whole different ballgame. I can't give you an answer until I discuss it with the chairman of the board. I can tell you now, I'm not in favor of it. It pushes us too far beyond our experience."

A project like this one may have ten subcontractors. Two or three will make up seventy-five percent of the work. However, all the payments, inspections, warranties on the work, workmanship, permits, and approvals by the local officials become the responsibility of the general contractor, so the owner has only one company to deal with for the project. A management fee, usually a percentage of the total project, is added to compensate the general contractor.

Chapter 2

"I don't like it, Barry," I said the day I returned and met with the majority stockholder and chairman of the board. "It puts us beyond anything we've done before and certainly puts me beyond my experience and out of my comfort zone."

Barry stroked his chin. We had done a project in the UAE, the United Arab Emirates, before and other parts of Asia and Europe, but not as the general contractor. "How much do you think the whole project will be?" he asked slowly.

"About twenty million," I replied. This was over ten times our usual jobs.

His eyes grew wide. His face flushed. A smile instantly appeared. I could almost see dollar signs appear in his eyes. "Twenty million," he muttered.

"Barry, I'm against it," I insisted. I could see I was losing the argument and needed to put all the cards on the table. "The risk is too great. We have no experience with a job this complicated. There are so many unknowns. And it's in Saudi Arabia. Remember Mel Brown's Company just down the street? They went bankrupt trying to do business there. It's a different business climate. We could easily be tripped up by customs or requirements we're not even aware of. We've always been the subcontractor on jobs like this. The general contractor provides a cushion between the foreign company and us. With this job, we'll be the intermediary between the Saudis and the subcontractors. We'll be providing the cushion. We've never been in this position before."

I took a breath, then immediately continued. "It'll be expensive just to put the bid together. I'll have to go over there for who knows how long, meeting with the port authority, obtain surveys and soils reports, investigate housing for our crew as well as obtain bids from local contractors for the excavation and additional labor. There will be a major dewatering effort. The tunnels and pits will be less than fifty yards from the ocean and below sea level. We'll have to hold back the Persian Gulf while we build the pits and tunnels." I felt drained just thinking about how elaborate the bid would be, let alone building it if we happened to get the job." In a last-ditch effort, I tried a different tact, "Smart business, Barry, is knowing when to pass on a job."

Barry was deaf to all arguments. The carrot of twenty million dollars flowing through his company thrilled him. It was too enticing.

"I think we can do it," he slowly, softly said, nodding his head. "Do what you have to. Prepare the bid."

"Now boarding Delta flight three to London Heathrow airport," the announcement came over New York's JFK airport intercom. It was an overnight flight over the Atlantic. After a layover at Heathrow for a few hours, another flight would put me in Dammam, Saudi Arabia, past midnight. On landing, we parked on the tarmac. There were no jetways, so we deplaned via a mobile stairway. Then walked a hundred yards in stifling heat between two rows of soldiers armed with ~~AK-47's~~ assault rifles. After reclaiming my suitcases, I proceeded to the immigration and customs area.

"Open your suitcase!" barked the immigration guard. He dumped the contents out on the counter and began rifling through the pile of items. Not finding anything objectionable, he pushed the entire, ransacked pile and empty suitcase off the end of the counter onto the floor. "Next," he shrieked.

This was a reconnaissance trip to gather information about the site, subcontractors, suppliers, and the business climate. Harry James was to meet me there to help arrange meetings and contacts. To an American, the Middle East is a strange place. That first morning at 4:30, I was awakened from an exhausted sleep to a screechy, mournful wail coming from a 1950s-quality loudspeaker. I jumped out of bed, staggered to the window and peered out, expecting to see rioting or some other commotion. I saw only a few people wobble out of their homes towards the mosque. It was the morning call to prayers.

The internet was standard in all US hotel rooms in the mid-1990s, not so in Saudi Arabia. There were no internet hookups in the hotel rooms or in the hotel business center, which boasted of paper, pencils, and a copier. That was all. As I ate my breakfast of cheese and figs in the hotel, I mulled over my email dilemma. I had a dial-up 800-number that would connect me to the internet in the US. But even if I could dial the 800 number, there was no way to connect the phone to my laptop. There were no computer jacks on the phones.

I took the cord normally used to connect my computer to the phone set, cut off one end and stripped the wires bare. Then took two straight pins out of a sewing kit I traveled with, pushed them through the phone cord between the phone and the wall. I then attached the bare wires to the straight pins and checked to see if I was lucky enough to have pierced the right wires in the phone cord. After a couple of tries, I got lucky. I used this connection to send and receive emails on that first trip. I left the pins piercing the cord so I could use them again the next day hoping the maid wouldn't see them.

The internet was highly scrutinized and regulated in this part of the world. It allowed easy access to what the rest of the world was like. All my emails were monitored on that first trip. Any email containing a comment, pro or con, about religion or the country was deleted. It was not returned. It just disappeared.

I discovered the hotel maids were all men, as were the waiters and secretaries. Women are not allowed to work, except as a schoolteacher or nurse. I also discovered women are not allowed to drive or own property. Women are not allowed to sit in the public area of a restaurant. They had to sit in a back room.

The first meeting with the Saudi Cement Company was with Mr. Al-Garni, the chief financial officer, Mr. Deshpande, the lead engineer, and Mr. Al-Hossari, the project manager. I spent a couple of hours reviewing the specifics of the project.

"We've arranged for you to meet the company president, Mr. Showail," Mr. Al-Garni said at the end of our meeting. We walked to Mr. Showail's office, which was a large room used as a conference room as well.

"Bring coffee for everyone," he directed his secretary at the back of the room.

"Please, no coffee for me," I interrupted. "I'll just have soda or water."

"Oh, you don't drink coffee?" said Mr. Showail. "Then tea, tea for everyone."

"Please, no tea for me," I said. "I'll just have soda or water, thank you."

"You don't drink tea or coffee?" asked Mr. Showail. "Why not?"

"It's for religious reasons," I said hesitantly in this strange setting.

"What religion won't let you drink tea or coffee?" he demanded.

"I belong to the Mormon Church, or you might…"

He cut me off mid-sentence, "I know the Mormon Church. You believe in polygamy. So do we," he said triumphantly. "Many of our young men go to your university in Utah to get their degree because your behavior standards are similar to ours."

Chapter 3

"Shall I order you a hooker?" Harry James said as we entered the restaurant. Harry and I were out for dinner after several long days of preparing and reviewing the bid for the project. It was a relaxed restaurant right on the Persian Gulf. It was interesting to be eating dinner while watching huge oil tankers stream by only a hundred yards away. A relaxed evening was much needed after being focused on a bid that was much more extensive than anything I had prepared before.

"What?" I asked, not believing what I was hearing.

"Shall I order you a hooker?" Harry asked again. "See, they have them here. Would you like one?" he said pointing to a tall, smoking contraption sitting on some of the tables. I had never seen one before.

"You call those things a hooker?" I asked very clearly to be sure of what he was talking about.

"Now, I hear you say it, I see where the problem is," he said chuckling and shaking his head. "What I said was hookah, not hooker. Shall I ask for a hookah?"

"Thanks for the offer, but I don't smoke," I said amused, and relieved. This was my third trip to Saudi Arabia in two months. Between getting bids from the subcontractors and the travel and the pressure to not overlook items that were out of my normal bidding experience, I was exhausted.

Harry spoke good, gentleman's English but still had a slight Iraqi accent, making a few words hard to distinguish. Harry was never in any of the meetings with Saudi Cement. Yet, he knew everything that was discussed. We often met immediately after a negotiation meeting where he reported their reaction to the various parts of the discussion and how to move forward in a favorable light. He would receive a commission should we be awarded the project. He knew little of construction costs or methods but was very helpful in steering me through the cultural and personal side of these negotiations.

"Can I take your order?" asked the waiter in almost perfect English.

"I'll take tea," replied Harry, then nodding towards me, "What would you like to drink?" When we would meet in the US or Europe, he would always have wine. Then I remembered, alcohol is not allowed in Saudi Arabia.

"I'll have a coke with ice, please," I replied. Ice in one's soda is a Western cultural tradition. Most of the rest of the world do not drink much soda, and when they do, it's usually warm.

It was a velvety evening, warm, and humid. A striking difference from the summer weather in Idaho where the air is dry, and jackets are needed as soon as the sun goes down. Though there were a few new foods like hummus and lots of figs, the food was generally very good. But there was no pork chops or bacon. Muslims don't eat pork.

"Saudi Cement will decide who will be awarded the contract by the end of their week, Thursday," Harry commented as we neared the end of the meal. "They've eliminated all but you and one other company."

Suddenly, the restaurant went dark except for a couple of night lights. The waiters, managers, and some of the patrons got up and quietly walked out.

"What's happening?" I asked, a little alarmed.

"Relax," Harry calmly said. "It's evening prayer time. They have to shut down for about thirty minutes and go to prayers."

"They just leave those eating and walk out?" I asked in astonishment.

"They even lock the door on the way out, Harry explained. "This is normal. We just sit and wait."

"Do you have a gut feel if we'll win the contract?" I asked. Harry usually had some inside information, and I thought he would have a good idea who would win the bidding.

He smiled a sly smile that slowly turned into a broad grin. "The two final bids are remarkably close in price. So, it will probably come down to each bidder's strong points and weak points." He paused for effect, then said, "So I added a little bonus that should tip the scales toward us." He paused, then continued, "Three hundred Viagra for the managers," he said as he chuckled.

I was stunned. Viagra had been on the market only a few months but had quickly become its own currency.

"Mr. Al-Hossari would like you to add a little bonus as well," Harry said. "He would like a Mercedes Benz E-Class to show up in his driveway. He is getting close to retirement and would like to go out in style."

"Harry, did you say 'bonus' because I heard 'bribe'," his smile faded.

"You have to remember you are not in America," Harry argued. "Business is often done this way here."

"Our company has never paid a bribe," I said. "No matter what country we're in."

"I'm sure you have often thrown in a few perks to grease the wheels, to improve your chances with a customer," Harry reasoned. "I'm sure you have given away hats or jackets. That's one end of the scale. Moving up the scale, perhaps you have paid the plane ticket to fly a potential customer to tour a job he was interested in. You probably even picked up the cost of his hotel and meals. You should look at a Mercedes the same way."

"We shouldn't even be bidding this job, let alone paying a bribe to get it," I argued back. "They wanted an American company to be the general contractor. The policy of this American company is we don't pay bribes! So, on the issue of the Mercedes, tell Mr. Al-Hossari he's out of line for even bringing it up. If that costs us the job, so be it."

Chapter

"We'll build it for twenty million, even. That's the lowest I'll go," I said. I was exhausted after showing up four hours earlier, having been told they would accept our 20.4-million-dollar bid. I would learn the pleading was never over with this company. They were continually requesting, arguing, even begging for additional items to be included without paying for them.

"Let's sign the contract," Mr. Showail, the company president said as he walked into the room. At some predetermined signal, the other six company men felt they had extracted all possible concessions. This last hammering had persisted for hours.

After the thirty seconds it took for Mr. Showail and I to sign the contract, "I must go," he curtly said. I thought it strange there were no celebrations, no congratulations around the room, no shaking hands. The atmosphere quickly went from one of negotiation to one of demands. By signing the contract, we had become their servant and were immediately treated as such.

"We want the rebar in the domes to be premium, epoxy-coated rebar," demanded Mr. Al-Hossari.

His request surprised me. We had used epoxy-coated rebar on several seaside projects before. It is no small item. It's expensive and not something you just throw in as a perk. If he knew they wanted epoxy-coated rebar, why not state such in the specifications of the bid?

"I'll be happy to work up a change order and submit it for your consideration," I said, trying to keep the meeting as mellow as possible.

"No," shouted Mr. Al-Hossari. "There will be no change orders on this project. We have signed a contract, and we expect it to be included in the contract."

"The contract you signed specifies regular rebar," I said with as much nonchalance as possible. "To upgrade would cost around two hundred thousand dollars. We can't; we won't provide epoxy-coated rebar without a change order."

"There will be no change orders!" repeated Mr. Al-Hossari. "We have signed a contract."

To avoid an argument within minutes of signing the contract, I stoically said, "We will be ordering the rebar for this project in about thirty days. I will submit a change order showing the added cost. If the signed change order is not returned by the time we order, the rebar as specified in the contract will be ordered."

I looked around the room. We were meeting in a conference room at the Ritz-Carlton Hotel in Vienna, Austria, a luxury five-star hotel. This hotel was picked to suit Mr. Showail. It was a striking scene of six Saudi Cement managers and engineers huddled together in a tight bundle on one side of the double table. On the other side of the table, I stood alone. Not having a Dome Technology team at the meeting, no doubt bolstered their demands.

Several times during the long, arduous bidding process, I had asked Barry to send someone with me. I needed backup to help keep track of the numerous discussion points and details. This project was ten times larger than anything we had bid or built before. We were operating as the general contractor, a position our company had never undertaken before. We were in a strange country where the customs, social norms, business climate, and political landscape are completely foreign to our company and me. Barry refused to send additional help. I never knew why. Perhaps he felt the company was too busy with other ongoing projects. Perhaps he felt like we didn't have much of a chance of getting the job, so why waste resources? Did he not realize if we failed on this project, he was risking his entire company? The customer and every subcontractor would turn into an enemy, fighting over the remnants of his company.

We had built domes in many foreign countries before, communist countries, countries in poverty, countries where corruption was the norm. In all those countries, at least there was an atmosphere of cooperation, of working together to complete the project. I would much rather conduct business with a communist than an Arab. At least a communist's attitude is conducive to getting the job done.

The battle lines had been drawn.

Chapter 5

Soon after being hired at Dome Technology, we built five domes in Murmansk, Russia. Murmansk is in the extreme northwest corner of Russia above the Arctic Circle and near the border with Finland. It is the seaport for much of Russia's nuclear fleet. The job had already been sold and was preparing to mobilize. It was my first experience in dealing with a foreign country.

"I know you've managed companies before but not a construction company and not doing business overseas," Barry said soon after I started with the company. "To help you learn the business, I'd like you to handle all the paperwork for the six truckloads we'll be shipping to Russia with our equipment and materials. You'll need to compose the manifests, import documents, and make shipping arrangements including inspections. That will keep you busy for the next couple of months. Randy will be the superintendent on the job. He'll be taking his family with him—his whole family."

I tried not to react to that bit of news. I couldn't help but marvel at the undertaking. Randy is Barry's younger brother. He has six kids, the youngest still in diapers. Not many would be brave enough to take a large family to work and live in that unknown environment. Most of one truckload would be food, diapers, and medicine for his family and a small crew going with him.

"I'm not leaving Tampa until I have a check in hand," I said to Bob Knight a couple of months later. Our packed containers had been shipped to Tampa, Florida, where they would be joined by over twenty containers from Bob's company and shipped to Murmansk. Knight Industrial was the general contractor on this job. "I've inspected our shipment and verified everything we agreed to supply is ready for export. As per our agreement, we are to be paid seven hundred thousand dollars before it leaves the country."

"We're still fabricating the last of the equipment our company will ship," Bob replied, fidgeting in his chair. "It'll be a couple more days before we're ready to ship. You best go back to Idaho. I'll send the check as soon as we're ready."

"I'm staying here in Tampa," I said firmly. "I'll be here every day until I have a check in hand. If I leave Tampa without a check, our containers leave with me. Receiving a check for seven hundred thousand dollars is the only task I have right now."

I was at Bob's office at 8:00 a.m. every morning for the next two weeks. But finally, I had a check in hand and was on the plane back to Idaho.

Chapter 6

"A bomb exploded onsite today," Randy reported one morning on the phone. We were several months into the job in Russia. Of course, we were alarmed and puzzled because his voice didn't convey the concern I'd expect. In fact, he seemed a little amused by the incident.

"Why do I feel like there is more to the story?" I asked.

"It was an old, World War II bomb that had been buried," Randy continued. "They were driving piles to support the foundation with a sixty-year-old crawler tractor with a pile driver mounted on the side."

When the soil is not solid enough to support the weight of the building, a common practice, especially at seaports, is to drive cement columns down in the ground to support the weight.

"The bomb was about twenty feet down in the ground," Randy continued. "When the cement pile hit it, it exploded. It blew the five-thousand-pound cement column up in the air and tipped the crawler tractor on its side. The operator was thrown clear. He was bruised up but otherwise, not hurt."

"Wow!" I said. "How long is that going to set us back?"

"Ha!" Randy chuckled. "They're already back operating. As soon as it happened, they brought out a bunch of equipment, tipped the tractor upright again, dozed in the crater left by the blast and started up again as if nothing had happened."

"Did you get any pictures?" I asked.

"No. They're pretty strict about pictures, being a naval port area," Randy explained.

"How's your family getting along there?" I asked.

"Good, generally," Randy replied. "There was an incident last week that was telling or rather amusing. I'd sent my three oldest boys to another part of town to see what they could find for tools, you know, hammers, pliers, clamps. We may run short before we are done. However, on the bus, they were acting like teenagers, joking and laughing. Also, on the bus was one of the Russian project managers. He came to me the next day, as serious as he could be."

"Go on," I said.

"He asked, with a great amount of concern, 'What's wrong with your kids? Do they have an illness?' What's sad is the people here have been repressed so long, they are very withdrawn. As they walk down the street, no one looks up or will look you in the eye. They walk along staring at the ground."

"Another oddity," he continued. "Instead of having a big clock in the town square, they have a meter that shows the current level of radiation. Because the naval fleet here is nuclear and all the ships leak radiation, they monitor the level of radiation in the city. When it gets too high, they send part of the fleet out to sea."

"That's got to be a big concern for the sailors stationed on those ships," I commented.

"Because of that, the pay is higher than most other jobs. What's worse," he explained, "They dispose of their nuclear waste by sending barrels of it as far north as possible then dump it. Once you get assigned to one of those ships, your life expectancy is less than ten years."

"It's hard to imagine they put up with that," I said.

"But there is a wait list to be assigned there," he said.

"Why? I don't understand," I said.

"In addition to higher pay, the government agrees to pay their families should they die while assigned there. Most of those on the wait-list are family men. The compensation means the family will never have to worry about affording food again."

Chapter 7

"I'm sending a sample of the cement they are providing us to build this project," Randy's voice came over the phone. "I'm sending it by FedEx. It's not setting up right, and I want our engineer to run some tests on it to see what we've got to work with."

"Give me details," I pleaded.

"Normally, we can add more concrete after it cures for a day. But we're finding this concrete won't hold up in that amount of time. The concrete used the previous day is collapsing."

"I've got the results back from the engineer's testing," I started the conversation with Randy a week later. "The reason it's not set in the normal amount of time, it's not ground nearly as fine as it is in the United States."

"That explains it," responded Randy. "Will it reach the needed strength eventually?"

"Yes, it will," I replied. "It will just take longer." "I'll complain to them, but I doubt it will make any difference," Randy said. "It means we'll have to build two domes at the same time and alternate between the two to add concrete."

"That means you'll have to use the spare set of fans we sent for a backup," I said as we talked through the problem. "And you won't have a backup if one fails."

"How fast can you get more fans here so we have a backup?" asked Randy. "I know we've got another set here in the yard."

"I'll get the fans moving today," I said. "A set of fans with motors weighs close to a ton. Shipping them expedited air freight could run fifteen to twenty thousand dollars. Because they are supplying concrete inferior to US standards, they'll have to pay the extra expense. I'll back charge the Russians. If they had let us known about the difference in concrete beforehand, we could have anticipated the problem at little additional cost."

The inflator fans used were custom built by Dome Technology for their type of construction. The components, off-the-shelf fans and motors, were common. But the way they were paired and assembled was proprietary. Being able to operate and adjust to a wide variety of circumstances was a major component in the success of the company.

The difference between an Arab's and the Russians' mentality was highlighted by how they responded to the cost increase. The Russians understood and accepted the change order without a whimper. Saudi Cement would whine and complain throughout the project, exacerbating the difficulty.

"Linden, let's go to my office," was the first thing Barry said as he met me at the door one morning. "There is someone there you'll want to talk to."

We walked to his office in silence, but I could see by the grin on his face he was amused about something. "Hi, I'm Linden," I said as I greeted the man in Barry's office.

Both Barry and the man broke out laughing. "This is Randy!" Barry said between chuckles.

I was shocked speechless. Randy had left to begin this project looking like the Pillsbury doughboy and returned looking like Arnold Schwarzenegger. I didn't recognize him. "You look great!" I stuttered. "You must have worked extra hard over there."

"It was that and the food," Randy replied. The food was horrible. The whole crew suffered. We ran out of Imodium. It was so bad. It was in the contract that the men could eat at the port cafeteria. But the food was bad, greasy, and poorly cooked. We rationed the food we had shipped over for my family as best we could. All the men lost a lot of weight."

"I was anxious to get my family home and into school," Randy veered off into another subject. "The whole crew came home except for Butch Maupin. It'll take another week or so to be sure our equipment is on the ship to be returned. I left him with about eight thousand dollars cash to grease the wheels. The Russians are very capable of accomplishing almost anything you need if they have the right incentive. The van we had shipped over presented a problem when it was time to leave. It was vital during the project. We used it for everything. We even stacked wood on top to haul back to the domes to burn and try to heat up inside the domes to speed up the curing process."

"Is there a problem with shipping it home?" I asked.

"The van served us well. But at this point, it is junk," Randy explained. "It barely runs and is beat up almost beyond recognition. But we will have to pay four thousand dollars duty if we don't re-export it."

"Can't we just abandon it somewhere out in the county?" Barry asked.

"If the Russians don't see it loaded on the ship and mark it as re-exported, they'll charge us," Randy responded.

"I have an idea," I started. "Have Butch go to the ship's captain. Explain that the van is junk and barely runs. Load the van onto the ship for re-export. Tell the captain, it's worth five hundred dollars to him if the van never reached Antwerp, his next stop. Emphasize to the captain we have no interest in seeing that van again." This solved the problem.

Frogs and Scorpions

A few months later, we sold a job to build several domes in Riga, Latvia. It had only been a year since the breakup of the Soviet Union. Latvia, a former Soviet Union State, was struggling to be its own country. Most of the managers of the various companies were Russians and carried on most of the communist methods and traditions.

I was in Riga a few months earlier to negotiate the contract. The high-rise hotel was a holdover from the Russian days. The rooms were sparsely furnished with only a thin mat on a concrete ledge for the bed. The décor was black—black carpet in hallways painted black. The lights were simple, dim bulbs that gave the feeling of walking in a cave.

"How depressing," I commented to Barry. Since I hadn't worked for the company very long, Barry accompanied me on this trip.

"The luggage boy told me there is a casino in the basement," Barry said. "I'd like to go take a look after we get some dinner." After dinner, we passed two guards with rifles at the stairs and two more guards with rifles at the base of the stairs at the entrance to the casino. The casino was a stuffy thirty-by-thirty-foot room with a few slot machines, a roulette table, and a poker table.

After the contract was signed but before we shipped any items, I went to back Riga to verify the site was secure and that the materials they were to provide were onsite. The site manager informed me I would have to obtain a port pass before being allowed onto the building site. He would need my passport to secure such a pass. This is common. I pulled out my passport and held it out for him.

He hesitated several seconds staring at my passport. Then gently, almost reverently, took it with both hands, stared at it some more, then held it high above his head and announced to the room, "Ah, an American passport. What everybody wants."

The bulk of the materials they were to provide consisted mainly of five truckloads of rebar. They were not on site when I arrived. I told the site manager I was going to stay until the materials were on site, and I could inspect them. We were ready to send our men and equipment to start building but would not until I could confirm the proper rebar was there.

"We should have the materials tomorrow," their site manager told me. The next day, still no rebar.

Finally, after ten days of delay and still no rebar, I delivered an ultimatum. "Our company cannot wait any longer. If the rebar is not onsite tomorrow, I'll return to the United States. We'll schedule another project ahead of yours. In three months, perhaps you'll be ready."

The Russian paced back and forth stuttering. Finally, taking a deep breath, he stopped pacing and faced me with a determination I had not seen before. He declared, "The rebar will be here tomorrow. We know where it is. We will get it tonight!"

The next day, two guards armed with machine guns, paced around a newly acquired pile of rebar.

Every project has unforeseen complications and difficulties. But even in poor countries and countries with governments and lifestyles unlike our own, solutions are found, progress is made, and the project is completed to the satisfaction of both parties. I found this cannot be assumed with some Arab countries.

Chapter

8

"The United States sent their women to beat Saddam Hussein," the port director joked as we sat in his office getting acquainted. The port at Dammam, Saudi Arabia, had been a staging area during the Gulf War in 1990. Tanks, artillery, trucks, and the needed supplies and support personnel were shipped in and made ready to deploy to neighboring Iraq. Working alongside the male soldiers were female soldiers. When the Saudis saw this, it became a common joke that the US had sent its women to fight the Iraqi leader.

"Never bring up any subject that could be construed as even remotely political," I said to Larry Bateman as I briefed him before he left to be the superintendent on the project. "Among the Saudi population, there are as many cheering for Saddam Hussein as there are cheering against him. You never know who is in favor or who is against. If they bring it up, which they often do, be careful to express a middle-of-the-road opinion. You are not there to have a political opinion. You're there to build a cement export terminal."

Zeid Jalil was the manager of Tamimi Trading and Contracting Company. This Saudi subcontractor would be used to provide most of the labor and subcontract work needed on the job. We often met or went to lunch or dinner as we discussed the needs and progress of the job.

When the discussion of work-related items finished, it was natural to wander to personal subjects.

"You have twin boys?" I asked.

"That's right," Zeid responded. "They're sixteen and starting to think seriously about college."

"What would you like them to study?" I asked.

"Engineering. They're not sure what field yet," he replied. After a pause, he continued, "I would love for them to study in America. I would give anything and everything if they could get a US student visa."

I was surprised at his strong feelings. "Why study in the US?" I asked.

"The US represents the best of everything," he said. When it comes to education, lifestyle, or just learning about life, the US is the best place to go for the most complete and the best there is."

"What's the chances they'll be able to go?" I asked.

"Poor," he replied. "My wife is Saudi, but I'm from Jordan. My boys were born here, but they're considered mixed blood, which all but eliminates them from consideration."

I felt comfortable in bring up a sensitive subject, religion. "I'm Christian. Most of our company is Christian. Do you have any reservations about doing business with Christians?"

"Not when it's profitable," he said with a smile.

"Why is there such a vast difference in what we believe?" I ventured further into sensitive territory.

"It all goes back to the Prophet Abraham," he said. "Are you familiar with the Prophet Abraham?"[2]

"Of course, in the Old Testament," I replied.

"Do you remember Abraham and his wife, Sarah, had no children and they were getting old? So, Abraham took Hagar, Sarah's servant, as another wife who bore Ishmael. Some years later, Sarah got pregnant and bore Isaac. Arabs and most Muslims are descendants of Ishmael, Abraham's firstborn by his second wife. But Christians are descendants of Isaac, Abraham's second son but by his first wife, born after Ishmael. It's a question of who has the rightful birthright? The firstborn by the second wife or the second born by his first wife?"

After meeting about the project, having dinner together, and a lengthy amount of small talk, we had been together several hours. I hesitated before asking the next question, fearing he may be insulted or at least resistant to answering it. "Muslims have very strict moral beliefs," I began. "What if one of your twins got a girl pregnant? What do Muslims believe in a case like that?"

He answered slowly but without hesitation, "I'd have to kill him. I wouldn't want to, but I'd have to kill him." His answer stunned me. Zeid is a Muslim. How devoted, I am still learning. He is also a family man. I could see his love for his family.

One evening after our usual meeting, he wanted to show me, or rather show off his favorite mall. The dazzle and glitz far exceeded the Crossroads Mall in Utah, The Mall of America in Minnesota, even 5th Avenue in New York. We ran into his wife and twin boys also at the mall. Zeid suggested we all have dinner at a nice restaurant there.

At first, his wife wore the traditional burka. Other than her hands, the only thing showing was her eyes. Zeid told me later that whenever he picks up his wife from teaching school and the female teachers emerge, he cannot pick his wife out. He must wait for her to come to find him.

As the dinner progressed, she excused herself to go to the restroom twice. Each time she came back, she had removed a bit more of her burka until her face and head were totally uncovered. Apparently, she was comfortable with me being in their group.

Chapter

9

"Do you think you can find a job for me?" the man at my office door asked. I looked up and was surprised to see Doug DeRoche. Doug had worked for the same construction company since high school. He had worked his way up to be their top superintendent, mostly building federal highways and installing utility lines.

I was surprised he was looking for a job. The company he worked for was a large, family-owned, regional company with a stellar reputation. But often in family-owned companies, promotions don't go to those who are talented and hardworking. Rather, those positions often go to family members. Right or wrong, there is often a parting of the ways by those who put in the tedious, day-to-day hard work that builds a successful company.

It didn't take long for me to realize a man like Doug was just what I needed to free up time and relieve some of the travel burden. "Yes, I think I have something," I replied. "Sit down, and I'll explain what I've got. See if you're interested." Doug was the kind of man who would run a job without any handholding. He took the bull by the horns and did what was needed to get the job done. He understood the economics of construction better than most accountants.

"Are you up for some travel?" I asked.

"Sure. I've been traveling my whole life. How long will I be gone?" he asked.

"The question you should be asking is not 'how long' but 'how far'. The job is in Saudi Arabia," I explained. "You'll be working out of this office but will need to go there about a week per month for progress meetings with the owners and to make sure the job stays on track."

Doug swallowed hard. He was used to going toe-to-toe with federal highway inspectors, city officials, and hardcore men who made their living demolishing buildings and highways. But Saudi Arabia was a different "kettle of fish," as Harry James would say.

"I…I'll give it a try," Doug stuttered. "I need a job. Do you think I can do it? What about the language? What language do they speak?"

"English is the official commercial language," I explained. "Everything dealing with the project is in English. And all their managers speak pretty good English. However, all the specifications are metric."

"Federal highway contracts are all metric," Doug said. "I'm comfortable with that."

"You've run jobs as the general contractor before," I continued. "You have some experience with that. I haven't nor has this company. To get the job, we had to bid it as the general contractor. Barry insisted we bid this job as the general. The thing that concerns me is the Saudis don't operate as if they're obligated by a contract. In the US, contracts are binding and enforceable. I have never dealt with a country like Saudi Arabia. We've built domes in Russia, Latvia, and other communist, former communist, and Third World countries. I would rather build anywhere than in Saudi Arabia. I know it sounds like I'm trying to talk you out of accepting the job, but I don't want you to be surprised. You'll need to be familiar with the drawings and what we're building," I explained. "Besides managing the project, your main job will be managing expectations."

"Expectations?" he questioned.

"Trying to enforce the terms of the contract as a legal document is futile. It would be too expensive for a company our size to try to enforce it overseas."

"So, what good is a contract?" Doug asked.

"We can perform the work as they've agreed to in the contract, but they will pressure us to do something different than what is specified. There will always be contract changes during a project, agreed upon changes. You know, change orders. But the Saudis refuse to agree to any change orders. They want to make additions to the contract without a change in the price. I've refused to make additions without a signed change order. They are not used to the push back. I've made some enemies because of that."

"Before the ink was dry on the contract, before we left the room, they were whining, complaining, and arguing to change the expectation of what they had just signed. I need someone who can move ahead with the scope of work while maintaining control, regardless of their whining and bellyaching. It's exhausting. I've needed some help in that area, but Barry has refused to give me any. I get the feeling he's scared of them and is reluctant to get involved."

"You paint an interesting picture. It'll be quite different than what I'm used to, but I'll give it a shot. When do you need me to start?" he asked.

"Today," I responded. "Bring in your passport, and I'll apply for your visa. That usually takes a week. As soon as it's here, we'll leave. I'll introduce you to the crew, the subcontractors, and the owners. We'll take what time we need in Saudi Arabia, probably three or four days. In our travels, we'll stop and meet Franz Aumund in Rheinberg, Germany, then Barry Mitchell of B&W Mechanical in England, and on the way back, we'll meet with several engineers for Fuller Material Handling in Pennsylvania. Those three companies are supplying and installing most of the equipment for the project."

Chapter 10

"How are you holding up?" I asked Doug as we walked into the Dammam Airport in Saudi Arabia. It was after midnight. It had been twenty hours since we took off in Idaho. Even at this late hour, the temperature was over a hundred degrees and near a hundred percent humidity. The aircraft parked a hundred yards from the terminal building on the tarmac in a row of airliners.

"When I saw the guards with the machine guns, I wondered if I was in the right place," Doug answered.

Two rows of guards lined the route leading from the plane to the terminal. Each carrying a rifle in case anyone was tempted to bolt before going through immigration. With the heat, humidity, and jetlag, just making it to the terminal building was punishing.

"When we go through immigration, prepare yourself for the rudest inspection you'll ever have," I explained.

Acting disgusted, the inspector dumped our suitcases out on the counter and threw the empty cases on the floor at the end of the counter. After a few minutes of rifling through the items, he pushed the pile off the end of the counter onto the empty suitcases and jerked his head to one side indicating we were done.

As Doug and I grabbed our clothes from the pile and stuffed them back into our suitcases, I quietly commented to Doug, "That was an improvement from the first time I went through here."

"How could that be an improvement? I've never been treated so rudely," he said.

"The first time I came through, they took my laptop and all my computer disks to another room. Then took twenty minutes looking at the disks and hard drive to be sure there was nothing that would defile the country. Welcome to Saudi Arabia."

"Do they all treat you like that here?" Doug asked as we were briskly approached by three taxi drivers as soon as we stepped out of the immigration area.

I quickly looked them over, sizing up which one looked the least devious. "We'll go with you," I said pointing to one of them. The selected driver quickly took a suitcase from each of us, establishing himself as the winner of this round of competition and walked towards his car in the parking lot.

"I have found most Saudis to be very considerate and hospitable," I explained. "But there is a striking, stringently adhered to class system here. What class you're in can change from building to building, even room to room depending on who else is in the room with you. What we just experienced is a good example.

"What do you mean?" Doug asked, a bit perplexed by this country and its customs.

"In the immigration area, the guards and inspectors have the power," I explained. "They assert this power by treating you badly. We submit to their authority by acquiescing to their bad treatment. When we left that area, we were approached by the taxi drivers; the roles were reversed. We now had the power because we have money to pay them. When we picked one, he immediately became our servant, and that's how he acted."

"It may take me some time to get used to all this," Doug commented as we rode towards the hotel.

"The lowest class is women, all women," I continued. "They are lower than servants. I have a hard time with that."

We pulled up to the hotel. I counted out fifty Saudi riyals, paid the driver, and we checked in. I'd kept several hundred riyals from the previous trip to pay taxis and airport tax until I could visit a bank to exchange more dollars into riyals.

"I was relieved to see you had some Saudi money for the taxi," Doug said in the elevator on the way up to our rooms.

"Use a credit card for all you can, but you'll need some cash for things like taxis and tips. The Saudi riyal is quite stable. One riyal is worth about twenty-five cents," I replied. "I'll meet you in the restaurant at ten in the morning. Since it's past midnight, sleep in and try to recover a bit from the jet lag. And pay no attention to that pathetic wailing you'll hear over loudspeakers in about three hours. It's the first call to prayers for the day."

Chapter 11

"What? No bacon for breakfast?" Doug sarcastically asked the next morning while looking over the menu.

"And you won't find any ham or pork chops here either," I replied.

"It's kind of slim pickings," he continued. "Fruit and cheese are supposed to fill me up?"

"And coffee," I replied. "Saudi Arabia is famous for coffee."

"That does no good for us milk drinkers," he offered.

"Men who stay here in this hotel don't know what a shovel looks like, let alone how to use it," I added. "They spend their days behind a desk and on the phone, so most eat little breakfast. I've got a car scheduled to pick us up and take us to the Saudi Cement office. I'll introduce you to the managers and explain why you're here."

"Why am I here?" Doug asked. "I mean, just what is my job description? And do you always use a car to take us around?"

"A car and driver here are cheap," I answered. "About twenty dollars per half day. I found you've got enough on your mind without worrying about finding your destination and getting jammed up because you don't know the local traffic laws. There are no street addresses here. When we mail documents or drawings, the address is just the company name and the city. FedEx and DHL keep their own list of companies and how to find them. Our crew has rented a pickup you can use as needed when you're here for several days."

"Your job description," I continued, "is to keep me from hearing about any problems or disagreements you or the crew may have here." My answer was a little facetious but generally accurate. "Larry Bateman is the job superintendent. I know you've worked with him before and know his capabilities. Ten months of sales effort and negotiations with the Saudis, as well as the mechanical suppliers, then drawings and finally, negotiations with the subcontractors have brought us to this point. The actual construction is just beginning. We still have a long way to go. I'm exhausted. I'm looking to you, Doug, for a little relief. Eat up. We've got a big day ahead of us and a lot of people to meet."

"Thanks for dinner, Mr. Jalil," I said as we left the diner with the manager of the major local subcontractor for the project. He would supply most of the labor and much of the equipment needed. "We've had a long day and are anxious to go to bed early to get over this jet lag. Would you drop us back at our hotel?"

"There's a new shopping mall I'd like to show you on the way back to the hotel," he answered. "It's very modern and right on the way. It'll just take a few minutes." Mr. Jalil was anxious to show off his modern city to his visitors. The mall proved to be like any new mall in the US, except there was much more shiny gold used in the storefronts. The products were mostly Western products from the US and Britain.

"The mosque where we pray is just across the street," Mr. Jalil said as he pointed the direction. "Tomorrow is our Sabbath." He then added to clarify, "Our Sabbath is your Friday."

"I think we've hit our limit for the day," I said wanting to head off any other detours or delays.

"Tomorrow after prayers, there will be a beheading," he announced in a tone one would use to announce a party. "Would you like to come?"

Shocked, Doug and I looked at each other. It took a few seconds, but I finally managed to stutter, "I…I think we'll pass."

"I understand," he casually said as we got in the car.

—⚬—

The day before we were to leave on the return trip, I scheduled a car to take us to the Saudi Cement manufacturing plant, a two-hour drive into the interior of the country. The trip had two main objectives, for Doug to meet Mr. Al-Hossari, the project manager over this terminal and to give ample time to hear what Doug thought of the job.

Mr. Al-Hossari was a crusty project manager nearing retirement and determined to go out making an impression. It was impossible to discuss details with him. He argued with everything anyone else said, even his own people.

"There are two things we're particularly at odds with Mr. Al-Hossari, even before we turn a shovel of dirt," I explained in the car as we sped by miles of barren sand dunes. "I refused to order premium epoxy-coated rebar for the project without a signed change order. We need to place that order soon to have the rebar here when we need it. He keeps asking. I keep refusing."

"That's reasonable," Doug said. "What's the second thing?"

"He insists we throw in a new Mercedes for him for awarding us the contract," I answered. "It's a bribe, a payoff. Apparently, that's a common practice here. I've refused, and he is not happy about it. According to Harry, he feels it's owed to him. He's been with the company over thirty-five years."

"Tell me more about Harry," Doug asked. "I've not met him. What is his role?"

"Harry is our agent on this job," I replied. "He brought us the job and made the needed introductions. I've never had an agent who operates like Harry. He was never in any of the negotiations, but he usually contacted me on the way back to the hotel or that evening. He could repeat everything that was discussed as if he were sitting in the room. He reports what was accepted, what they had a problem with, how to address the problem, and what to bring up in our next meeting.

He won't tell me how, but somehow, he was listening in on the whole meeting. As we are paid, he receives a portion of his commission. To a large degree, we owe getting this job to Harry."

At the Saudi Cement manufacturing plant

"Would you like a fresh fig?" asked Mr. Al-Hossari. "We grow them here onsite using the wash water from the plant." We had had a tour of the plant, which was scurrying from one building to another to avoid the hundred fifteen degree heat. The offer of the figs was made as we stood up to leave. Acting gracious for the offer, we each took a fig, took a small bite so we could say we tried them, shook hands and headed for the door, discarding the rest of the figs as soon as we were in the car.

"I've never cared for figs," I said relaxing in the car which the driver had left running the whole time to keep it cool for our return. "Even fig cookies, I never cared for. Fresh raw figs are much worse."

"I agree," Doug said as we settled in for a monotonous two-hour ride back to the hotel. "Mr. Al-Hossari brought up the rebar again. When I said that would require a signed change order. 'We have a signed contract. No change orders' he keeps repeating."

"Just keep telling him that without a signed change order, we'll use exactly what's in the contract. And if other engineers or managers are in the room to hear it, that's even better. I can't decide if that's an item he forgot to include in the specs, or if he just thought he could bully his way into getting it after the contract was signed."

"Have you heard the story about the frog and the scorpion at the Nile River?" I asked

"I think so, but remind me," Doug answered.

"A scorpion asked a frog to carry him over the Nile River," I began. "The frog was afraid of being stung, but the scorpion argued that if it did so, both would sink and drown. The frog consented to the scorpion's request, but midway across the river, the scorpion does indeed sting the frog. Dooming them both. With his dying breath, the frog asked, 'Why?' The scorpion replied, 'You knew what I was when I crawled on your back.' I'm finding that working with the Saudis is a lot like that story."

"If it's any of my business, how is the company paid on this job?" Doug asked.

"It is your business," I replied. "I'm glad you asked. I've probably spent as much time on the payment arrangements as on contract details. We're paid through a Letter of Credit." I could see Doug question how a Letter of Credit applied to our contract. "When we reach a milestone, we submit a notarized document stating we have reached a certain milestone and request the payment attached to that milestone. Their bank pays our bank the predetermined amount. After our bank takes out their handling fee, the rest goes into our account. The amounts to be paid at the milestones are all detailed in the Letter of Credit. We've only made one application for payment so far, shipment of the air-form, equipment, and other supplies from the US. The payment process went smoothly."

"What if they disagree with the amount being requested?" Doug asked.

"As long as the statements and documents are in order and have the proper wording, their bank is required to pay us. That is the only part of this whole agreement I feel is written in our favor. If they disagree, they must wait until after we're paid to initiate a claim or make an adjustment. If there are change orders or adjustments, the Letter of Credit must be amended before payment amounts can be changed. How many projects have you run where there have been no change orders?" I asked.

"None," Doug responded immediately. "Change orders are often the bread and butter for a contractor."

"Right," I replied. "I get the feeling the Saudis think they've been bitten a few times by change orders. That's the only reason I can see why they're so determined not to accept any. But change orders can reduce the work and price as well as increase it. The Letter of Credit must be amended to reflect the change."

We rode in silence the rest of the way, mulling over the contract, the work, and the attitude of the Saudis. The car that came that day was a twelve-year-old Chevy Caprice. Even though the interior was worn, it had been well maintained, and it rode well. The air conditioning was top-notch, no small item considering we were speeding through barren sand dunes at eighty miles per hour where the temperature was pushing a hundred fifteen degrees. That year's model was some of the largest produced before high oil prices forced models to downsize. Doug and I rode along comfortably in the back seat, not having to pay attention to the road, which was straight and flat.

After twenty minutes of riding in silence, I suggested, "Perhaps their attitude regarding change orders comes from the fear that adding money to a negotiated contract may get out of hand and put their jobs in jeopardy. Next time they ask for something which would normally require a change order, let's consider approaching it another way. On a project this size and this complicated, there are always areas that could be economized, reduced, or even eliminated. Offer to reduce or change the scope of work to offset the upcharge for the change order. That way, we can grant their request without changing the bottom line. It would still need to be written down and signed, but it would show zero monetary impact. I would never trust a simple verbal agreement with this company. Use our standard change-order form. Just be sure they sign it before you actually change the scope of work."

Doug just nodded, saying nothing. He had negotiated a thousand change orders in his career. I'm sure some of them were in a hostile situation with a customer. I was optimistic his experience would prepare him for dealing with this customer, a customer who was unlike any I had dealt with before.

"After all, 'We have a signed contract,'" I said mocking Mr. Al-Hossari.

Chapter 12

"It's not safe where you're living," the consulate official emphatically said to Doug and Larry. They were visiting the American consulate to report where they were living and how many Americans were with them. "You need to move to a compound where expats and their families stay. Here's a list of several to consider. Be sure to report back to us where you move to."

"Annoying and hostile!" Doug vented to Larry as they left the consulate. "This country is annoying and hostile. You learn to dance around all their weird customs to get the job done— stopping work several times a day to pray, a different weekend than the rest of the world, and the hideous garb their women must wear. On top of that, you must guard your life! It'll be remarkable if we make any money on this job."

"I don't watch much TV," Larry responded, "But I guess I'll have to start watching a local newscast to keep up on what is happening, an English newscast if I can find one."

"It's part of the job," Doug replied. "Part of this job, anyway."

Weekends took some getting used to in Saudi Arabia. The Muslim Sabbath is on Fridays. Thursdays are days when some companies work and some do not, like our Saturdays. At times, there were fifty local workers on the project. Their custom was to work a half day on Thursday and none on Friday. In the States, our men are used to working a half day on Saturday and none on Sunday. Larry and Doug worked it out the best they could.

Once, while I was in their country over their Sabbath, I wanted to get a feel for what a more affluent neighborhood was like. I left the hotel and walked a short distance to such a neighborhood. The homes were all surrounded by thick, high stone walls. Through the iron gates to the property, I could see elaborate homes with little or no landscaping. Water for plants or the lawn had to be recycled water, so most yards were left in sand.

After walking about an hour, I found a spot where the high stone wall shaded the sidewalk. While I sat on the curb, only two cars happened to pass by. Both cars stopped and invited me to their home for dinner. I happened to be sitting in front of one of their homes. They were quite cordial and were at ease chatting a few minutes about why I was in town.

Not knowing anything about them, I declined their offers. But I admired their genuine hospitality to a stranger in their town.

"Driver, you sit in the back. Mr. Fielding and I will sit up front," the Saudi sheik said. "I want to drive." Then as we got in his top-of-the-line BMW and fastened our seatbelts, he added, "These drivers they send me are usually too timid. I need to get there."

The Saudi sheik I had my appointment with owned a large construction company and held a position in the community. Harry James had arranged the appointment. When we start a project in a new town or country, I take the opportunity to raise interest in our domes with other companies in the area. We had arrived at his office on time but waited about thirty minutes for him to appear. When he did, he apologized for being late and asked me to ride with him to his next appointment. We could talk in the car.

Just as the Arab closed his door, a skinny, ragged young man about thirty years old with a young boy about eight, walked up and weakly said, "Can you help us? My son and I haven't eaten for two days. Could you spare enough to help us get something to eat?"

I looked on, expecting the Arab to ignore or dismiss him. After all, he was late to an important appointment. Instead, the Arab looked over the man and his son carefully, took out his wallet and handed the man a thousand riyals, the equivalent at the time of about two hundred fifty US dollars. I was astounded. He then said, "Come to my office the day after Holy Day at 9:00 a.m. Tell them I have a job for you. I or someone else will instruct you where to start work." I was surprised at the extra time he took, even though he was late.

He was not a timid driver. We passed through a small settlement where there was only a four-way stop. After a brief stop, with cars at each of the four stop signs, he announced, "I'm going," as he floored the car and sped through the intersection. "I have found," he then explained to me, "if I am bold, the others generally will wait." He then added, "Occasionally, I have to slam on the brakes, but not often."

"Please fasten your seatbelts and prepare for our descent into London," the pilot announced over the intercom. We had departed Saudi Arabia just before 2:00 a.m. and was scheduled to arrive in London just after 7:00 a.m. This was a typical schedule when traveling to or from the Middle East. The flights would arrive in Saudi Arabia in the middle of the night, refuel, board new passengers, and depart for European cities. Flights would arrive in Europe just after sunup in time to make connecting flights across the Atlantic. Sleep was useless even on the Boeing 777, the newest model on the market and the epitome of luxury. You're trying to relax but remain alert enough so as not to miss an important announcement, such as bad weather, a diversion, or some other interruption to the schedule.

Long-range traveling is brutal. It looks luxurious and appealing, but it's the most grueling part of the job. You constantly must be on high alert. Schedules, flights, or gates can change. If you miss something, you end up stranded and delayed, scrambling to reconnect to where you're going. While traveling, your life is a mixture of acute boredom punctuated at any second with the high anxiety of an unexpected event.

The flight was smooth and quiet. As we began our descent from thirty-eight thousand feet, I glanced down and noticed we were descending into a thick bank of clouds. After continuing to descend for thirty minutes, I began to get a bit anxious anticipating seeing the ground but continuing in thick clouds.

I was stunned by the sudden, unmistakable bump of the plane touching down on the runway. Looking out the window, the fog was still so thick I could not see the wing tip. The plane continued to slow, making the usual reverse thrust to slow us down. Eventually, the plane came to a complete stop before proceeding very slowly to a taxiway. The pilot came on the intercom and said, "Because of the thick fog, we have just made a completely unassisted computer landing."

As we deplaned, I said to the pilot, "That landing was amazing."

Lowering his voice as if he was taking me into his confidence he said, "These new planes are something. You really only need one pilot and a dog to fly one." I looked puzzled, begging further explanation. He continued, "You need the pilot to communicate with traffic control, and you need the dog to bite him if he tries to touch anything."

Chapter 13

"I never envisioned such a massive hole," I remarked to Larry onsite shortly after construction started. "I knew the dewatering operation would be significant, but I never realized it would take up most of the site."

"This close to the ocean, the water table is just below ground level," Larry began reciting the salient points of why the excavation was so big. "We have to pour the concrete for the foundation at the bottom of the bucket elevator thirty-five feet down. The whole Persian Gulf is trying to drown us. To keep the sides from caving in on us, we must taper them back three feet for every one foot deeper we dig. We end up with a hole over two hundred feet across to pour a ten-by-ten-foot slab for the elevator to sit on. The tapered sides of the hole are covered with a network of pipes and sucker tubes to suck the water out of the soil as it approached the hole from the ocean. It takes vacuum pumps, positive pressure pumps as well as back up pumps to put the water back into the Gulf."

"We are essentially recycling the water back to the Gulf," Larry continued over the racket of the various pumps and engines. "Even so, the port authority insists we take three water samples a day of the water going back into the Gulf to be sure we're not picking up any contaminants in the process."

"I'm glad I've got you two here to stay on top of this," I said to Larry and Doug.

"This isn't that much difference from what I've been doing in Idaho," Doug responded. "The biggest difference is instead of pine trees, deer, and elk for scenery, we've got sand dunes and camels. This environment, this culture is new to both Larry and me. If the Saudis will stay out of our way, I'm confident we can get the job done."

"Let's go back in the office where it's quieter and cooler," Larry said. "I had one of the foremen of the subcontractor ask me something yesterday I want to talk to you about."

Back in the office, we each took a chair and positioned it to take maximum advantage of the stream of cool air from the airconditioning vent.

"I had one of Tamimi's foreman come to me quite upset yesterday," Larry began. "He said his wife had been diagnosed with a tumor on her pituitary gland."

"That's too bad, but what does it have to do with us?" I asked.

"He says they don't have the medical expertise here for the surgery needed to remove it. And even if they did, it would be too expensive for him to afford."

"Again, that's too bad, but what does it have to do with us?" I repeated.

"He's sure we have that capability in the US," Larry continued. "He is asking us to help him find a doctor that does it. He can pay her plane ticket to the US, but he'll need help in paying for the surgery."

"He doesn't have insurance?" I asked.

"He's Jordanian," Larry explained. "Native Saudis have government health care paid for by their oil money. Being Jordanian, he must buy his own insurance, which he and most others working here don't do. The Saudis do provide them with basic medical needs, antibiotics, check-ups, and so on. But this is far beyond that."

"This is an unusual request," I said. "But I'll make a few calls when I get back home and see if I can turn up anything."

After the request was made to find some medical help for the wife of the worker who was suffering with a tumor, I made some calls and talked to a neighbor, who was a doctor, about the request. The neighbor did a brief search on the internet and even made a call to a doctor who specialized in the procedure.

Based on the limited information available, the doctor concluded that such a tumor is usually not malignant. However, to remove it required a delicate operation. The doctor, who was based in Phoenix, even offered to perform the surgery at no charge if they could get the woman to Phoenix.

In just a few days since making the request, Larry was able to report back to the crew foreman our success in finding a doctor who was willing and able to do the surgery. On hearing the news, the man shed tears at the thought of strangers ten thousand miles away willing to help his wife.

"You care for my wife more than I do," Larry reported the Arab saying as the latter wiped tears from his eyes.

I was beginning to understand why the Saudis insisted on an American company to be the general contractor on this job. By employing an American company, the Saudis were able to tap into American resources, even resources unattached to the building of a cement export terminal. Most Americans are more than willing to share our technology, medicine, innovations, and expertise with other countries of the world.

More important than the abundance of natural resources, America has an abundance of opportunity. This abundance, plus the ability to innovate, has resulted in being the richest country in the world. Even the Saudis want to tap into that.

Chapter

"Nobody important will ever be down there," shouted Mr. Deshpande, one of the Saudi engineers who was over the machinery. "Let's move on."

We were discussing ventilation in the tunnel that would run under the storage dome. The tunnel housed the motor, cement pump, and other machinery to move the cement powder to the ship. The motor to move the cement powder would be a large motor, over three hundred horsepower. Should the motor or other equipment in the tunnel catch fire, what would be the best design to remove the smoke and heat, give the best chance of survival and escape should someone be down there at the time? This was the question that had dominated the discussion for the last hour. Mr. Deshpande wasn't interested in the question of survival of the common laborer.

Others from Fuller, the supplier and installer of the equipment, were there. After a period of shocked silence at such a statement, I said to the supplier, "Apparently you and I can make this decision outside of this meeting." The message was clear. The value of human life varied greatly depending on your class.

Doug and Larry stood watching the crew of nearly thirty men place rebar on the inside of the dome in preparation to cover it with a layer of concrete shot into place with a high-pressure concrete pump.

Depending on the building's use, engineering dictated anywhere from one to six layers of rebar, each layer covered with concrete. The placing of forty-foot lengths of rebar is the most tedious and time-consuming step in building the dome. Several crews worked at a time out of specially designed baskets mounted on a crane arm or on long-reach forklifts.

"Larry, notice the man on the right end of the basket," Doug said. "After a few minutes, you'll realize he's doing twice the work as the others in the basket. But he also keeps urging the other on, to keep up with him."

The next time the basket was lowered to take on another load of rebar, Doug walked over to the man, took out his wallet, and handed a dollar bill to the man. "Keep up the good work," Doug simply said. Of course, the man couldn't understand what Doug had said, but he understood the dollar bill. The man beamed as he showed the others in the basket.

Doug handed out dollar bills several more times over the next few days as he saw workers who worked harder than the others. Predictably, production improved.

About a week later, Zeid pulled Doug aside, "I'd prefer you not hand out those dollar bills." After a moment of confused silence on Doug's part, Zeid continued, "It upsets the pecking order."

"Just that simple act has improved our production by over twenty-five percent, Doug argued. "How can that be bad?"

"The increased production is good here at work," Zeid replied. "But it carries back to their living quarters and social interaction. It's causing some problems when they're not at work."

"I see your point," Doug said. "But there must be some way to reward good work without causing problems."

Doug quit giving out dollar bills. Instead, he would hand out a new pair of work gloves.

In Paris, where the next progress meeting was held

The Saudis liked to meet in Europe especially during the summer. It was cooler, plus it gave them the opportunity to access items which were illegal in Saudi Arabia, items such as alcohol, newspapers, and TV shows not available within the "Kingdom." They also enjoyed the French food. I saw no hesitation to partake of all these items when outside their country.

Doug and Larry Bateman met me in Paris to participate in the meetings. "Let's see if we can find a place for some dinner," I said to them after the meetings had finished for the day. We found a little café that looked inviting. We had a tasty, enjoyable dinner catching up on things back home since Larry had been away from home for several months.

It was the height of the summer heat. Parisians tend to be stingy with their air conditioning. We were all hot and sweaty and drank many refills of Coke with ice. When the bill came, we were shocked to see the amount for the Cokes alone was twice the cost of the meals.

"I guess they don't have free refills in this country," I said as I picked up the bill intending to put it on a company credit card.

"No way!" Doug interrupted. "That's embarrassing. I'll not let the company pick up the tab for my Cokes." He pulled out his wallet and handed me several bills.

In addition to alcohol and a very liberal society, Paris is also famous for sculptures and other art that would be considered too risqué or even unlawful in Arab countries. The Louvre, the Rodin Museum, and dozens of other museums and exhibits occupied any free time we had. I was fascinated by the city and made a mental note that after the project was over, Ann and I should spend a week's vacation there.

Chapter 15

"Mr. Showail wants to meet at his home for the progress meeting this month," Harry James said over the phone. I had arrived at 2:00 a.m. the night before as usual. Harry got right to the point without any small talk. He was already in the country and had been in contact with the Saudis. "A driver will pick you up at 10:00 a.m. and take you to his house. Plan on a short meeting and a little lunch after the meeting. I'll call again after the meeting." Harry hung up.

On arriving at Mr. Showail's home, I was greeted by a male servant. "Follow me. Mr. Showail will meet you in the pavilion."

I felt like the route we took to get to the pavilion was intended to show off the fine home. I enjoyed the tour. No expense had been spared to achieve its opulence. Gold, marble, crystal, large paintings, and other museum quality items were everywhere in its lavish interior. It reminded me of an early 1900s mansion depicted in a movie, only modernized.

The pavilion was an elaborate party tent. Couches with many pillows encircled the perimeter. The floor was covered with a puffy mat. Everyone had their shoes off. There were five or six others there from the Saudi company. A table was set up with coffee, tea, lemonade, ice water, and an assortment of cookies. We all helped ourselves as we sat and chatted, waiting for Mr. Showail to enter.

"What is happening in America?" was the first question Mr. Showail abruptly asked as he entered the room. The question was urgent, steeped in anxiety and uncertainty. His face was contorted as if he feared for his life.

"What do you mean?" I asked slowly. I had not realized how much the rest of the world relies on the United States for stability and direction.

"The election!" he shouted. "Will there be an uprising, a coup, a revolt?"

At first, I thought he was kidding, making a joke, but soon saw the genuine fear in his eyes and words. It was November 2000. The election between George W. Bush and Al Gore was so close; it was still unclear who the winner would be two weeks after the election. Al Gore was narrowly ahead in the popular vote, but George Bush was ahead by one vote in the electoral count. It came down to one state, Florida, which was also so close. A hand count of about forty-five thousand paper ballots was ordered. The news was filled with talk and arguments over hanging chads, a ballot that had been punched but not completely and pregnant chads, ballots that were dimpled but not punched.

The hand counters were trying to interpret the intention and mindset of the voter from the appearance of the ballot. Thus, several weeks later, the election was still undecided and the world quivered. It quivered not because of the closeness of the vote, but because it feared this brutal test of the world's premier democracy would spawn unrest, and the situation may dissolve into anarchy which could easily spread to other countries.

Finally, the issue was argued before the US Supreme Court, which ruled the hand count was unconstitutional because it held a few counties to a different standard than the rest of the State. It ordered the original machine count to stand which gave George W. Bush the advantage and the election by the slimmest of margins. George W. Bush won with two hundred seventy-one electoral votes, giving him a one-vote majority.

There were a few demonstrations but no riots, no revolt, no revolution. The United States had weathered the crucible of extreme division.

"I see you are building the domes with standard rebar!" complained Mr. Al-Hossari. This was how he opened our next monthly progress meeting. There was no greeting, no welcome, no acknowledgment of the ten-thousand-mile flight to get here, no small-talk, no discussion about the latest political events.

"We are using the exact rebar specified in the contract," I replied. "You had the opportunity to upgrade the rebar with a change order. But that window is past."

"We have a signed contract. There will be no change orders," Mr. Al-Hossari repeated.

Mr. Al-Hossari only occasionally led the monthly progress meetings. Little was accomplished when he was in attendance. Usually, there was a discussion about world events. Oil prices were often a topic. Since oil prices peaked at a hundred twenty dollars a barrel in the late 1970s, they had fallen steadily and are currently in the low thirty dollars per barrel range. A monthly payment to Saudi men is dependent on the level of oil revenue.

Before the election, US political scandals were a favorite topic for small talk before project discussions. The Monica Lewinsky-Bill Clinton scandal was of particular interest. Even the stained blue dress was discussed and how such a powerful man could be caught up in such an affair that had become public. It was a soap opera being played out on a global stage. Many Saudis closely followed the daily episodes detailing the latest developments.

Chapter 16

"What's happened, Doug?", I said as I glanced up to the door of my office. Seeing Doug standing there. Something serious was on his mind. He leaned against the door frame looking down at the floor, a sour look on his face. I could almost see the lightning and thunder of a dark cloud gather around him. This was uncharacteristic for Doug.

"What's gone wrong?" I prodded.

He took a deep breath, paused, and finally replied, "The job is fine." There was another pause, "I ran into my old boss over the weekend."

"And?" again I prodded.

"He offered me my old job back."

"That's bad only if you took him up on it," I said to encourage more information.

"He said that the reason I had to leave in the first place is no longer an issue. And they need me."

"It's not bad to be in demand," I said. "It's a good thing for you, but a bad thing for me. I'm guessing you took him up on his offer?"

"He offered me my old position and even a modest increase in salary. I'm not a guy who will jump ship and leave a guy mid-job for two bits more. The truth is, I've never had to go ten thousand miles to run a job before. And I'm finding it tough. I've dealt with a lot of knotheads before too, but none like the Saudis."

"I thought I was the only one who thought that", I answered. "Come in, and sit down, and let me try to wrap my brain around this development."

"I'm not totally surprised by this," I continued. "The travel is grueling. And the abject disparity between the two cultures piles on an additional layer to an already difficult job. You've done a great job here. And you've giving me a badly needed breather. You showed up at just the right time. I was barely hanging on between putting the bid together, negotiating with the equipment suppliers, and starting the job in a strange environment. All of which put me way out of my comfort zone."

"I feel like I've just been operating outside my abilities," Doug responded. "Like I was always off-kilter and trying to get back on track but never could. I feel it's an opportunity to go back to a job I'm familiar with. A job I know what to anticipate, where I can feel at ease."

"Consider the points you can add to your resume," I replied. You now have global experience. You've mobilized into an airport crawling with soldiers carrying machine guns. You've helped build a seaport, something you'll never be able to say while working in the Rocky Mountains. And you've learned how to ride a camel."

Doug smiled and nodded as he said, "I'm glad you're taking this good."

"We're close enough to the end of the job, I won't try to replace you," I said. "Larry and I will muddle through the best we can. How soon will you be leaving?"

"They want me as soon as I can button things up here," Doug answered.

"Schedule a call with Larry for tomorrow with you and me at this end," I explained. "You can explain everything that is ongoing. I've got a progress meeting with the Saudis in Genève in two weeks. I'll have Larry fly up to meet me there for those meetings."

"I am going to miss jetting around to all those exotic places, Paris, Geneva, Amsterdam." Doug commented. "It is interesting and a little bizarre, but now I can say 'I've been there, done that.'"

"When you came to work here, I needed someone who could take the reins and manage the ongoing details on his own," I explained. "You were able to do that, even though this job was different then a highway or a utility line. I hate to see you leave, but I'm glad you were here for a long as you were."

Chapter 17

"Larry, get me to a hospital," I weakly said. Larry and I had flown into Geneva for progress meetings with the Saudis. We met up at the hotel and found a place to eat. It was a buffet type restaurant. It's hard not to pile on more than you should, trying as many foods as possible from the ample selection.

After dinner, we returned to the hotel and tried to overcome the jetlag, which always follows a transoceanic flight. I got sick shortly after returning to the hotel. I vomited until there was nothing left. The floor was wet with profuse sweat pouring off my face. I began drifting in and out of consciousness when the phone rang. It was nearly midnight.

"I'm sicker than I've ever been," I interrupted Larry's reason for calling. "You've got to get me to a hospital."

"I'll call a taxi," Larry responded. "If you can make it to the front desk, I'll meet you there and get you to a hospital."

Now, with a goal to focus on, I was able to pull on some clothes and meet Larry at the front desk. The taxi was there as soon as we were ready.

The emergency room wasn't busy, so I was evaluated and an IV started as soon as I arrived. For the next several hours, blood was drawn, X-rays taken, several different doctors examined me looking for the cause of the illness. After several hours, the extreme nausea relented, and I was able to relax.

"Our diagnosis is you had a bad case of food poisoning," the doctor said in the morning. "We found nothing of concern in the blood test or X-ray. How do you feel?"

"Much better," I manage to respond. "I'm still woozy, but the nausea is gone. That was the worst I've ever experienced."

"You were severely dehydrated," explained the doctor. "We'll keep you here another couple of hours and continue the IV to help you rehydrate. If you still have no nausea, you can then be discharged."

Other than being very weak, I felt fine as I approached the clerk to settle my bill on being discharged. "I'll have to just pay what I owe and settle with my insurance when I get back to the States," I said to the clerk.

"This is unusual, but I understand," she replied. "I'll print your bill." She fussed with the computer and printer a bit indicating it was unusual for one to simply pay their bill in full on being discharged.

After several minutes, with bill in hand, she timidly said as she laid the bill on the counter, "Will you be able to handle two hundred thirty-six dollars?"

"No problem," I replied with a sigh of relief. I was expecting much more.

"I'll take a taxi to the airport and catch a flight home," I said to Larry on the phone after being discharged. "They said it was food poisoning. I'm weak as a kitten and in no condition to face the Saudis. Take good notes. With Doug gone, I'll want to review everything they brought up in the meeting."

"You had me worried," Larry said. "You were so pale and lifeless. How did they treat you? How was the bill?"

"I was prepared for a hefty bill considering blood tests, X-rays, IVs, and exams by at least two doctors," I said. "The bill came to only two hundred thirty-six dollars."

As soon as the wheels were off the runway, I pulled the blanket over me and went to sleep.

"Sir, we're about to land," the stewardess said. "You've been asleep since we left Geneva. You even slept through meals."

Chapter

18

"Barry, I want you to double my current salary," I stated as firmly as I could. The Saudi project was proceeding. Problems were being handled. The frequent trips required were punishing. I hardly had time to recover from one trip before another was expected.

The Letter of Credit was working well as a method of receiving payments. In turn, we were paying the suppliers and subcontractors. To handle the dramatically higher cash flow, I had negotiated a much higher operating line of credit from Merrill Lynch in Chicago.

"I'll think about it," Barry slowly said, not completely surprised and trying to delay any response.

I anticipated his delay and was prepared, "This job is requiring much more than either you or I anticipated. If you put off an answer until the job is done and base your response on if we made a profit or not, that is unacceptable. As I told you before we even bid it, this job will reveal how much we don't know about doing business as a general contractor in Saudi Arabia. Just getting to the end of the job without a financial disaster is the goal now. I need to be paid what this job is worth to continue. I need your answer by five o' clock this afternoon, or you can finish the project without me." I left the room.

I had delivered an ultimatum, which should only be done if you're ready to accept the alternative. I might be out of a job the next day if Barry didn't agree. But being out of a job looked like relief. It beckoned to me when compared to continuing. To finish and close out the job would be a huge burden. I had to feel good about the compensation to continue.

I'm sure Barry felt I'd backed him into a corner. He didn't see that I also felt backed into a corner. Barry had built the business with a great amount of scraping by and sacrifice. It was hard for him to understand why his employees shouldn't sacrifice as well. As majority stockholder, any success would add to and remain in his net worth. Eventually, I would leave the company and that would be the end of any value I would receive from the company.

Several years earlier, we had completed a good year with a decent, legitimate profit. It was decided to bonus some of the superintendents. Barry asked if I would be interested in receiving a minority stock position in the company instead of a bonus.

Minority stock positions in a small company are worthless. Any financial returns or voting strength is still subject to the whims of the majority owner. I declined his offer in lieu of a cash bonus like the superintendents.

Barry wasn't in it for the money. He was in it for the experience, for the variety. "It doesn't matter if my idea doesn't make any money," he once said to me as we discussed a new idea. "What matters is how many things we can try."

Barry is an innovator. I often said if he didn't come up with three new ideas by lunchtime, he was dozing. He and his brothers had developed a method to build large, strong concrete domes that could span hundreds of feet beginning with a form held up by a small amount of air pressure. All the construction takes place on the inside. When completed, the structure has no internal bracing and can support heavy loads of machinery or even a control room on top.

But when it came to financial matters, he needed help. "What does amortization mean?" he once asked me as we left a meeting with our banker. We had gone to the meeting together so he could introduce me as the new general manager. That was the only time he was involved in the operating finances of the company while I was there. Barry was smart. He just had other things he'd rather learn about.

The division of responsibility was working well. He spent his energy developing or improving ways to accomplish the work. I was focused on financial and employee matters and sales. I thoroughly enjoyed the sales part of the job. To stand in front of a room full of engineers and managers in a posh, high-rise office building in a lavishly appointed conference room was a real kick. I enjoyed discussing the engineering and construction methods used in our buildings.

It was midmorning when I met with Barry and stated my request. The rest of the day was spent in a holding pattern. I addressed several items that needed immediate decisions but put off anything that could wait a day or two, anticipating leaving the job. I had accepted the likelihood that he would turn down my request.

"Linden, come to my office please," Barry said over the intercom at 4:55 p.m. I had been simmering on this all day from every angle I could think of. As I walked to his office, I was resolved that no matter what his response, I would feel better when I left. Either I would be relieved of the pressure I was under, or I would be paid more to help compensate for the pressure.

"I'll pay you what you asked for," Barry flatly said. He added nothing else, no preamble, no build up, no justification, no additional comments.

"Thank you," I said as I left his office.

Chapter 19

I was at my desk a few minutes before 8:00 a.m. The office was still quiet. The receptionist wasn't in yet. The phone rang. I noticed the caller ID. It was Larry at the Saudi job. Calls from him at this time of day were quite common. Ten hours difference in time zones put him near the end of his day and I, at the beginning.

"Hi Larry," I said as I picked up the phone. "How did the job go today?"

"I heard something today you need to know about." His voice quivered. "I was talking to our local subcontractor today, Mr. Jalil. He said Mr. Al-Hossari is telling people he will bankrupt us before we are done."

The relationship with the Saudi Cement Company had been rocky most of the project due mainly to them asking for additional work to be done above the contract without compensation. Of course, we would want to do the extra work, but they refused to pay for any added work or materials. Change orders are a common practice throughout the world and allows extra work to be added after the contract is signed. Extra compensation for the extra work is negotiated. The difference with the Saudi company was they refused even to negotiate added pay for the extra work. I was surprised he was so open about the effort to bankrupt us. And if he was so open about it, he must already have a plan of how to accomplish it.

In a mental flash of stark clarity, what had been bubbling just under the surface for months became crystal clear. The Saudis were determined to financially ruin us. In fact, they wanted to destroy us, to bankrupt us. Why? We insisted on sticking to the contract and being compensated for the extra work and materials they requested. We wouldn't give into their whining. But failure to achieve the added work made them look weak and ineffective to their peers and managers. They were not accustomed to the push back.

"Thank Mr. Jalil for alerting us," I responded to Larry. "See if you can find out if he knows what their plan is."

Our relationship with the subcontractor, Mr. Jalil of Tamimi Construction, had been good from the beginning. We had already negotiated the sale of all our onsite equipment to Tamimi, rather than pay for returning it halfway around the world.

Now that their intentions were clear, my goal was to extract our men from that country without damage. Normally, we would use a project like this to draw interest of other similar companies and secure additional projects in the area, not so in this case. I set my mind to crafting our exit from the region as quickly and as quietly as possible.

"Here is what I want you to do," I said to Larry the next day on the phone. "Finish the remaining items as quickly as you can. Do you think that will take about two weeks?"

"We should be able to do it in two weeks," Larry responded.

"Good," I continued. "Perception and timing are critical. I'll plan on your last day on-site will be in two weeks on Wednesday. Wednesday is important. Leave the country that night. "But!" I emphasized, then paused to be sure Larry was listening carefully. "You must make the Saudis think you've got at least two more weeks before you're done. Wednesday is important because it's just before their weekend. No attention will be paid to the project until they return on Saturday. That will give our crew time to get clear out of the country before they're aware of it."

"Okay," Larry responded hesitantly. "Any ideas on how I should do that?"

"Tell them there are some issues in the tunnel under the domes," I explained. "Make up an issue with the cement pump. Or tell them the hydraulics on the slide gates are not operating correctly, and you had to order some parts."

"That should be easy enough," Larry replied. "Why in the tunnel?"

"For some reason, the tunnels make them nervous, and they avoid going down there," I answered.

"That's interesting," Larry mused. "Now that you mention it, whenever a Saudi would come out to inspect the project, he always found an excuse to not go down in the tunnel."

I explained further, "In a meeting with Fuller, myself, and a Saudi, we were discussing where and how to install the exhaust fans to handle the smoke in the tunnel in the event of a fire in the pump motor. After about an hour of discussing the pros and cons of placing the fan in various places and whether it should be an exhaust fan or an input fan, the Saudi became irritated and frustrated. 'Let's move on! the Saudi yelled. It doesn't matter about the fan. Nobody of any importance will ever be down there anyway!'"

"I can't believe they said that" Larry said.

"Harry James admitted he had heard some grumbling among the Saudi managers and especially Mr. Al-Hossari," I continued. "He kept hearing two reasons for the Saudis negative talk. One, I refused to upgrade to premium, epoxy-coated steel without a change order."

"What was the second reason?" Larry asked.

"I refused to buy Mr. Al-Hossari a new Mercedes," I explained.

"What's the plan after we finish?" Larry asked.

"As you finish work on Wednesday night," I said, "tell the Saudis and Mr. Jalil's crew you'll be back on Saturday to continue work, Friday being their Sabbath day. Then leave Saudi Arabia that night and get to an airport in Europe out of their reach. Go to Amsterdam, Frankfurt, or London. I've learned the threat is real. If they can, they'll stop you from leaving."

"How will they do that?" Larry asked.

"They'll confiscate your passports at the airport. You'll essentially become their prisoners, and as such, they can make all kinds of demands before they let you go. That's how they plan to bankrupt us."

"Do you really think they would do that?" asked Larry.

"Saudi Arabia is essentially a ruthless dictatorship. Look on the internet," I said. "A Saudi oil company has already done just that to a British company. Now there is a big dispute about getting the British crew out of the country."

I paused for questions. I could tell he was a little shocked by what I was saying. There was silence.

"You've got to keep all this to yourself, Larry. Don't even tell our men until the day you leave. You need to be out of the country before the Saudis know you're gone. If you don't, or if word gets out you are about to leave, it could get very unpleasant, fast."

"At the same time, the day before their weekend, I need to draw the remaining funds on the Letter of Credit. We need to get those funds in our bank account before they know were gone. For this to work, we can't have a hiccup. Let's talk every day for the next two weeks."

Chapter 20

"What I don't say will be just as important as what I do say. Probably more important." I was talking to Gary DeGrange, the officer at the bank we had used to set up the Letter of Credit and receive payments from the Saudis.

"Okay?" Gary slowly said, puzzled by the way I started our phone call.

"We're finishing our work in Saudi Arabia in the next week or so," I explained. "It's critical the last draw on the Letter of Credit for the remainder of the project goes through without exception or question. With that in mind, I'll draw up the pro forma documents and email them to you for your review."

"I understand," Gary replied. "I'll watch for them, review them, and get back to you."

"The timing of the submission is just as critical," I explained. "It needs to arrive at their bank ahead of their weekend, enough time for them to review it and wire back the funds before their weekend begins."

"I don't understand," Gary responded. "We can't control how quickly they wire funds..."

"I know," I cut him off, not to be rude but to impress on him this was a critical issue. "The Letter of Credit gives them three business days to either wire the funds or file an exception. This will be the sixth draw on the Letter of Credit. Please look back at the previous draws and see what the usual turnaround time was." I paused a few seconds but continued before he could formulate a question. "This is where a bit of art in international cash-flow management is vital. I know you have questions as to why this needs to be so precise, so urgent. You are a bank officer, it's best if you're only concerned with the mechanics of the transfer."

"Now you're scaring me," Gary added.

"We are getting close to finishing our contract with the Saudi Cement Company. We need to secure the final payment according to the Letter of Credit as soon as possible, after we certify completion. It's also important that draw occurs on a Wednesday, just before their weekend—Thursday and Friday."

There was a long pause. Finally, Gary stuttered, "Okay. I'll get right on your pro forma docs as soon as they arrive."

"I'll have them to you within the hour," I replied. "It would be good if you could review them and reply with any corrections before the end of the day. You know they're not extensive, just a few sentences. But they must be perfect, not a period or comma out of place."

I met with Barry later that morning to explain what was happening, and what needed to happen with the Saudi Project.

"Remember about six weeks ago, the Saudis wanted to remove about two million dollars from our contract and give that portion to a local contractor," I started.

"Yes, I remember them taking some out of our contract. Remind me what they took out," Barry asked.

"It was the communications and equipment control package for the facility."

"Yes, I remember now. What about it?" he asked.

"Because they removed it from our contract, they should have issued a change order and the corresponding amount needed to be removed from the Letter of Credit," I explained. "In the past six weeks, I've sent four proposed amendments to the Letter of Credit and change orders for their approval. They rejected all of them, even when it would be to their advantage to agree."

"Why?" Barry asked.

"They gave no reason and made no counterproposal," I replied. "Here is what I think is happening. Mr. Al-Hossari, their project manager, is probably charged with making sure the amount of funds wired agrees with the progress of the project. I'm guessing he feels if he refuses to agree to any modifications, no funds will be wired, putting us in a real bind."

"Is that true?" asked Barry, sounding alarmed.

"No. Mr. Al-Hossari has no control if the funds are wired," I explained. "It's all in their bank's control at this point. As long as the documents are as specified in the Letter of Credit, the bank will wire the funds. The only way to change that is for both sides to agree to an amendment. And, without an amendment, the Letter of Credit is still for twenty million."

"What does all this mean?" Barry asked, agitated this explanation was taking so long.

"I'm working with our bank to make the final draw Wednesday of next week," I said. "It will be for the complete reminder of the Letter of Credit, about three million dollars, two million more than we have coming. At the same time, and this is critical, our entire crew will finish the job and leave Saudi Arabia that night. I'm trying to time the draw to be at the end of their week as well, so the Saudis won't learn about it until the first of their week, Saturday. By then our men will be out of the country, out of reach."

"What about our equipment?" Barry asked.

"We sold all our equipment that was on that project to Tamimi Construction, the local subcontractor, about a month ago rather than have to pay to ship it home," I reminded Barry. "Mr. Al-Hossari has been bragging to other Saudi managers he is going to bankrupt us before we leave the country."

"How could..." Barry started.

"By seizing their passports at the airport," I said. "Our crew would essentially be held hostage until we give in to their demands, which we have seen throughout the project will be unreasonable."

"They wouldn't do that," Barry objected.

"Saudi Arabia is essentially a dictatorship," I was getting worked up now. "US law means nothing there. Look on the internet. Seizing passports is exactly what happened to a British oil company a few months ago to keep them in the country. I've sat across the table from them and looked into their eyes. What I saw was terrifying. Ask yourself, are you willing to trust a country which beheads someone who is unfaithful in their marriage? Do you think they will go easy on an outsider, an infidel?"

Barry's eyes glazed over. I could see he wished he were somewhere else, somewhere not so complicated. Somewhere with a machine he could fix. This made no sense in his world.

"Keep your fingers crossed," I finally said. "There are a lot of dominos that have to fall just right in the next two weeks for you to save your company."

Chapter 21

"Barry, you will get a call on Saturday from somebody at the Saudi Cement Company. Do not answer the call!" I tried to impress on him the importance of that. "No matter how many times they call, do not answer the call. Do not speak to them. They will also call me. I will not talk to them until Monday. We can't talk to them until we know our men are safely out of that country, and we know if the last payment is in our bank. Then I will speak to them Monday morning. It's very important what is said to them."

Barry can be a bit dense and headstrong at times. I did my best to impress on him, this was a time he needed to take some direction. Barry is known as someone who does his own thing. Thinking outside of the box has served him well. In this instance, however, I needed to control the conversation.

The dominos fell precisely as planned, like a choreographed dance. I was feeling jubilant. Our crew finished the project, vanished from Saudi Arabia and were in London by Friday morning. The draw on the Letter of Credit went off without a hitch. The funds were wired and secured in our bank as well by Friday morning. Friday was a quiet day of celebration in our company.

As expected, calls from Saudi Cement Company started coming Saturday morning. Barry refrained from talking to them. Since our men and funds were now safe, I could have answered their calls, but a couple more days of hand-wringing would impress on them that we now had the leverage. Two million dollars of their money was in our bank. I slept well for the first time in two years.

Early Monday morning, the anticipated call came. I was still at home getting ready for work and happened to be outside starting the water on the lawn.

"Mr. Fielding, why did you…" the voice on the other end started.

"Stop!" I shouted. I was glad I was outside so I wouldn't disturb the rest of the family. "I know we have drawn more money than we are entitled to. We will meet you four weeks from today at the office in London. We will tell you then how much we are willing to give back. No one from our company will talk to you before then. Goodbye." I hung up.

"The Saudis have already called this morning," I said as I walked into Barry's office. "We'll meet them four weeks from today in London to discuss how much we'll return."

"Perhaps you should take a lawyer," he said.

"That's a good idea," I replied. "I'll contact the same firm in Salt Lake City that has done patent work for us. I'm sure they've got other attorneys who specialize in contract issues."

I paused, knowing the next thing I would say would not sit well with him. "Barry, you need to be at that meeting in London," I said firmly.

"You can handle it," he shrugged. "I don't need to go."

"Yes, you do," I insisted. "And I'll tell you why. You own the company. You need to be there so you can sign off on whatever the final number is. I know I have the authority to settle this. My intention is to resolve this on the spot and be through with Saudi Arabia. I don't want to return home and be second-guessed on something this important."

"Do you realize they are trying to bankrupt you?" I continued. "They want to destroy Dome Technology. They wanted to seize our men's passports, effectively holding them hostage until we give them whatever they want."

"Yes, you've told me," he said. "I just can't believe…"

"Believe it, Barry," I said emphatically. The frustration of being sent alone into a den of brutes was showing. "The only reason we can sit here now and talk casually about this is because we've gained the upper hand. Our men are out of the country. We have no equipment there. And we have a substantial amount of their money in our bank account. And if they want to see any of that money back, they have to behave. Imagine the panic we'd be in if our men were stranded there and they still owned us a million dollars?"

"They could sue us," he offered.

"They could, and it would be horribly expensive for both companies," I countered. "That's all the more reason for you to be there, to reduce the possibility of a lawsuit. It will be an unpleasant meeting. But you need to be there, not only to sign off on a settlement but to reinforce this is the end of our involvement in this project."

"You can handle it. I don't want to go," then he caught what he was saying. "Rather, I don't need to go."

I took a breath hoping it wouldn't come to what I said next, "If you don't go, I won't either. We'll default on the meeting which will enrage them even more. Your life will never be the same after that. And Barry, it will be the end of your company."

Chapter 22

"Let me review how I think the meeting will go," I said as Barry and I met with the Mr. Weathersby, the attorney selected to accompany us to the London meeting.

This particular attorney would give the perfect impression we needed in the meeting. He was large, tall, and heavy. He stood at least six foot four inches and weighed at least three hundred fifty pounds, maybe close to four hundred. He was in his early thirties. He spoke slowly and clearly. In previous meetings with the Saudis, there had always been six to eight of them, and me. We needed enough of a presence to ensure we kept the upper hand. Barry doesn't give a bold impression. He gives more of a Pillsbury-doughboy impression.

I continued my prepping. "We'll fly in the day before and stay in the Park Lane Marriott hotel just two blocks from the meeting," I could see Barry cringe when I mentioned the hotel. It was too expensive. "I picked that hotel because the meeting has to go off like clockwork, no traffic jams, and no trouble getting a taxi. Yes, it's a nice hotel, about five hundred dollars per night." Barry's eyes popped open wide, and his mouth dropped open. I looked directly at him and said, "Several million dollars and your company are on the line. This is not the time to squeak by. Get plenty of sleep the night before the meeting to get rid of as much jet lag as possible. Barry, you can't be dozing off during the meeting."

I continued, "I guarantee there will be some drama in this meeting. So, prepare yourselves. For several hours, the Saudis will recite complaints, details, chain of events, and perceived omissions. Anything we say during this time won't matter. It will be ignored. I'll try to limit any response to save time. They will be trying to impress each other as much as us. It will probably go past lunchtime. If it does, they'll break for lunch and have sandwiches brought in as they have in the past."

"At some point, and this is crucial," I paused to add emphasis, "I will slam my briefcase shut, state that we are leaving, stand, and walk out. That is your signal to gather your things and follow me out. There will be loud objections and a lot of whining. They will want us to stop and continue talking. Don't listen to them. I say again, do not listen to them. Ignore them and follow me out. Unless we leave the room, there will not be any progress made!"

"How do you know this?" the attorney asked.

"I've been in a hundred meetings with them," I answered. "This is their nature. This is how they negotiate. However, this time, we clearly have the leverage, all the leverage, and we must use it."

On the morning of the meeting, Barry met me in the lobby dressed in a dirty work shirt, pants and work boots covered with dried concrete and urethane. I asked Barry, "Is that the shirt you're going to wear to the meeting?"

Barry looked at his shirt and shoes, wrinkled his brow and shrugged his shoulders.

"I was afraid you'd wear a dirty shirt," I said a little disgusted. "I've got a new, clean shirt in my room. I bought it anticipating this. Come with me. We've got about three minutes to get you changed and leave for the meeting."

Chapter 23

"No!" said Mr. Al-Garni emphatically, "We will not allow your attorney in the meeting." The CFO of Saudi Cement had rarely attended progress meetings. But this meeting was to deal solely with money, so he was there to lead the meeting. He was accompanied by ten other Saudi managers.

"Mr. Weathersby is here to advise us, not you," I responded. "What if he agrees not to speak in the meeting? I mean, he will not speak to the meeting. If he has something to say, he will speak only to Barry or myself."

Several of the Saudi's bunched together and mumbled a few sentences in Arabic. "No, we still will not allow him in the meeting," Mr. Al-Garni stated.

"Then we will be leaving," I said, testing the strength of our leverage. "With no meeting, the current situation remains the same. Meaning, we will continue to hold your money."

"Okay," quickly responded Mr. Al-Garni, realizing he was not in a strong position, "But he must agree to limit his communication to you and Barry."

"I notice Mr. Al-Hossari is not here," I said as we selected seats on opposite sides of the large conference table. "As the project manager on this job, I expected to see him here for this meeting."

There was dead silence for an unnervingly long time as eyes on their side of the table darted back and forth, each hoping someone else would respond to the question. "He did not come," Mr. Al-Garni finally, curtly said. At the same time, there were various other mumblings heard, such as, "He did not come," and "These are financial matters," and "He was not allowed to come."

I learned later through Harry James, Mr. Al-Hossari was to monitor the payments to make sure they matched the amount of work completed. When payments were made from the Letter of Credit, he was the first one to review it. It then went to the financial department for booking. Apparently, Mr. Al-Hossari didn't understand that with a Letter of Credit he was approving the payment amount after it had been paid. If the amount paid was wrong, he would have to negotiate the return of the funds or a modification to the Letter of Credit adjusting for the error.

But Mr. Al-Hossari believed no payments would be made if he refused to accept the modifications for the previous reduction in the scope of work. He had not realized until a modification was agreed on, the schedule of payments would remain unchanged. He errored in that piece of his plan to bankrupt our company. When his error came to light after our final draw of funds, he was abruptly, quietly, and immediatedly required to retire from the company.

The meeting finally got underway. The entire morning was spent reiterating a laundry list of complaints that had already been addressed and resolved during the project.

Lunchtime was awkward. We moved to the lunchroom and sandwiches were provided. Small talk was difficult as we searched for a subject that wouldn't escalate into an argument.

After lunch, the simmering pot boiled over. "How could you overdraw two million dollars?" shouted Mr. Al-Garni. His pride had been badly wounded. Such emotional wounds are often worse than a physical wound with a bullet or knife. There would have been some honor in that type of wound. But this, in his mind, was treachery of the highest order. Veins stood out on his forehead and neck as he shouted. His eyes were bloodshot and buggy. He stood up from his chair and shook his fist. With every word, a spray of spit added to the verbal barrage levied at the three Americans across the table. Three

Americans verses ten from the Saudi Arabian company. They, the Saudis, had been outmaneuvered and outsmarted.

"Everything about the draw of funds was legal and in accordance with standing orders," I responded, trying to conceal any emotion. "The documents were scrutinized by your own bank as well as our bank." Then pointing my finger at him, I continued, "You allowed this to happen by ignoring an amendment to the Letter of Credit," I said staring directly at Mr. Al-Garni. Now I was getting revved up. "I submitted four modifications for you to review, and Saudi Cement rejected them all out of hand. No counteroffer was made, no comments on needed changes. I doubt if you even read them. Then!" I got loud, "Then when Mr. Al-Hossari started telling others he was out to bankrupt us, did you expect me to do nothing? We finished our scope of work and got our men out of the country."

My comments ricocheted off the walls leaving an eerie extended silence. The Arabs shriveled and sank down in their chairs under the piercing stare of the Americans. Some even put their hands covering their faces. This was the apex. The silence was deafening. The Americans clearly had the upper hand. Like cold rainwater seeping through a shabby roof, the Saudis slowly realized they would have to negotiate, not simply demand.

Their only pathetic response was to begin repeating grievances we had already heard for hours. I cut him off mid-sentence. "We came here today for one reason only," I began, "To discuss the issue of the funds we hold in our account. Every time we try to discuss those funds, you revert to issues either already resolved during construction or you failed to authorize with a change order. Clearly, you are not interested in reclaiming any of those funds. We are wasting no more time. We are leaving this meeting and leaving the issue unresolved." I slammed my briefcase closed, gave a nod to Barry and the attorney, stood up, and walked towards the door. Barry and Mr. Weathersby dutifully followed. Just before we walked through the door, to add some trepidation, I turned and said, "Good luck finding those funds. There are a lot of banks in the world anxious to accommodate a US company."

Chapter 24

"Wait. Stop. Sit down. We'll discuss money now," pleaded Mr. Al-Garni as we left the room.

"Keep walking," I said over my shoulder to Barry and the attorney.

"Please, wait. Stop. We'll get to the point now," Mr. Al-Garni continued pleading as he followed us out the door into the hall.

"Keep walking," I said again.

In desperation, Mr. Al-Garni pushed passed us against the wall, spun around, stood in the middle of the hallway, and put out both hands to stop us. "Please come back in. I b…beg you. Please come back in." He was a striking image, dressed in the usual Saudi white robe with a red and white checkered head dress held on by double black hoops made from goats' wool. "Come back in. I beg you," he withered.

I glared at him as piercingly as I could and said, "We will not go back into that room." I paused while staring directly at his eyes. Then continued, "We will, however, go to another room, the three of us. You have ten minutes," I said as I looked at my watch "And one chance to bring us a number, a settlement number. If we reject it, we will be out of the building with no further negotiations. If we accept your number, there will be absolutely no further negotiations. We will sign a statement of agreement, and wire the money when we get home. There will be no further contact with anyone in your company," I said as I pointed at him.

We were shuffled into another office and within a few minutes, a paper with one sentence scrawled on it was brought in. It said: Dome Technology to return $2,100,000 to Saudi Cement Company.

I read it, then handed the paper to Barry. He briefly looked at it then asked, "What do you think of this number?"

"2.1 million dollars will put us close to a breakeven for the project. 1.9 million dollars would give us a modest small profit, which would be nice given all the headaches this job has been. But 2.1 million dollars is not devastating. We would live to fight another day. And we can say we left Saudi Arabia with the company intact. A lot of companies can't say that."

"Do you have a pen?" Barry asked.

"I always carry a pen," I said handing him my pen.

He sat for a full thirty seconds, pen poised over the paper, then scribbled his name on the paper.

"This is exactly why you needed to be here," I said, "to sign the final settlement."

We were halfway back to the hotel before anyone said anything. Finally, Mr. Weathersby spoke up, "That was a meeting I'll never forget. Do you think you'll ever do business in Saudi Arabia again?"

"Never," I quickly replied. Then added after a breath or two, "I guess you should never say never. Maybe, after the hard lessons we've learned this time around, I might consider it again, under the right circumstances."

"The whole meeting went just as you said it would," commented Mr. Weathersby. "It's as if they were following your script or outline. How did you know that's the way it would play out?"

I simply replied, "A scorpion is always a scorpion."

EPILOGUE

The only reason we were able to leave Saudi Arabia with personnel unscathed and the company intact was we had maneuvered into a position where we were holding a significant sum of their money and only agreed to return it after they were forced to agree to a final settlement. During the project, Saudi Cement Company was given several opportunities to rectify the situation. Each time, they refused. I've puzzled over why they allowed themselves to be put in that position for years since then.

The CFO, Mr. Al-Garni, was a young, bright man who should have caught the need to change payment terms i.e., the Letter of Credit. However, Mr. Al-Hossari was the project manager. He had worked for the company for decades and had a reputation for being forceful, unbending, and uncompromising. Other managers in the company were content to steer clear of any oversight or question any of his pronouncements. One such pronouncement dictated immediately after signing the contract was: There will be no change orders!

When our scope of work was reduced by two million dollars, the Letter of Credit should have been reduced by a similar amount. Apparently, Mr. Al-Hossari viewed reducing the Letter of Credit, the amount to be paid to Dome Technology, as a change order and rejected it without realizing what he was doing.

Dome Technology had successfully completed other projects with countries whose business mindset is vastly different from ours—Russia, Latvia, South Korea, Jordan, even the United Arab Emirates.

The final settlement amount put Dome Technology near a breakeven for the overall project. Given the turbulence of the project, it could have been a lot worse.

NOTES

1. Chapters 5–7 may seem off-topic. They were included to illustrate most projects run into unforeseen difficulties. The difficulties were handled, sometimes requiring a change order and sometimes at extra expense solely for Dome Technology.
2. The Old Testament prophet Abraham is the common forefather of those of both the Christian/Jewish faith and the Muslim faith. Abraham and Sarah were childless, and Sarah was considered beyond childbearing years. Sarah encouraged Abraham to take her handmaiden, Hagar, as a wife in hopes of having a child, which he did. Hagar became pregnant and bore Ishmael. Thirteen years later, it was prophesied that Sarah would become pregnant. She laughed at the prophesy. She did become pregnant and bore Isaac when she was ninety years old and Abraham was a hundred. Sarah became jealous of Hagar and Ishmael and forced them from their household (Genesis 17–18).
3. September 11, 2001. Fortunately, the confrontation meeting with Saudi Cement Company occurred six months prior to the attacks on 9/11. The faceoff at that meeting severed all previous and future ties. The fact that most of the terrorist were from Saudi Arabia would have mangled any business matters there. I was in Baltimore when the attacks occurred. I wrote the following on the plane on the way home five days after the attack.

   As I write this, I'm on a flight from Baltimore to Atlanta then onto Salt Lake . It's Sunday, September 16, 2001. Last Monday, I flew to Baltimore for a meeting scheduled for Tuesday. I arrived at the hotel long after midnight due to several travel delays then went to bed. The meeting the next day wasn't till after lunch, so I slept late. When I got up, I spent some time getting ready

for the meeting. Later that morning, I dialed up to check email. There are always a few headlines that come up first on the home page. I was puzzled when I saw a picture of the first twin tower on fire with a headline about America Under Attack. My first thought was *What kind of sick joke is someone playing with the Internet? Has this site been hacked?*

At that moment, Kirby from our office noticed I had logged on and sent me an instant message, "Have fun getting home!" was all he wrote. I asked him to explain.

"Turn on your TV," he answered. I only had the TV on thirty seconds when the cameras caught the second plane, live, crashing into the second tower. I was stunned and found myself muttering to myself, "Is this real?"

As I watched for the next several hours, I saw the events unfold that we now have been seeing as reruns on TV hundreds of times—the towers collapsing, the people running, the huge clouds of smoke and ash chasing the running crowds of people in their suits and ties and nice dresses. And the pile of rubble that remained.

It was getting close to the time for my meeting. I half expected a call from the customer postponing the meeting, but none came. I was to meet with three engineers.

On arriving, we met, shook hands, made a few comments about the events, then silence. Four of us just stood in the hall and looked at the floor. Finally, the lead engineer, took a deep breath and just above a whisper said, "Just before you came, I learned my sister-in-law was on one of those planes. We'll have to reschedule the meeting. I'm sorry, but I'm leaving now."

Suddenly the events of the day took on even a more disturbing color. I now knew someone who had a family member taken from them. I left to anchor myself in front of the TV, watching for hours, hardly breathing. What will this mean? This is the beginning of a chain of events that there's no way of telling how involved or prolonged it will be. This will undoubtedly flavor our lives from now on. We will be less carefree. Traveling will not be so easy, cheap, and thoughtless. Suddenly, I didn't value all the free travel I've earned near as much. Last week, one of the safest places you could be was on an airplane. Once you drove to the airport, checked in, and got your boarding pass, you were "in the system." The airline had a responsibility to take care of you, feed you, provide a bed if your trip got delayed, to keep you safe, to even provide entertainment as you traveled. This week, the mole hill of risk has grown into a mountain, at least in our minds.

I stayed in Baltimore five days until planes began to fly again, and I was able to confirm a seat on a flight home. More than a few times I shed tears as I watched the story continue to unfold on TV. I snapped up the paper each morning and devoured each story. I received two emails of concern and condolence from men in Japan and Lithuania. I saw a full-page ad in USA Today proclaiming: THE PEOPLE OF KUWAIT SEND THEIR SYMPATHY," and again when I saw the leaders of our nation ask for divine guidance in the heavy, history-altering decisions that lie before them. American flags were flown from everywhere, on porches, draped on freeway overpasses, flapping wildly from being mounted in the back of pickup trucks and on car bumpers, and in a parking lot, a large crane with the boom extended hundreds of feet in the air displaying a large flag flying grandly on top.

This morning I got up at 3:30 a.m. to get to the airport. Due to extra security checks, we were instructed to be at the airport at least three hours early. When I walked into the ticket lobby at 4:30 a.m. there was already a mass of people with lines several hundred feet long winding back and forth then down a hall, leaving no more room in the lobby. The lines from the different airlines were intertwined, so it took several minutes and some trial and error to discover which line I was looking for.

Several people standing behind me in line noticed one man had been at the ticket counter trying to check in for about forty-five minutes. He looked Hispanic. He had papers and more papers spread out over the counter. The agent finally left and got a supervisor. A few minutes later a very large, dignified looking black man in a suit got involved. Then a uniformed security officer jointed the scene. A few minutes later, three more uniformed police officers joined the group. After a heated discussion, which included one of the officers yelling, "Where did you get these papers? These are not legitimate papers." They were joined by three more policemen, then the group led the man outside where he was searched, handcuffed, and stuffed in the back of a police car. It was rather unsettling.

After waiting in line about an hour, I saw on the monitor my flight had just been cancelled. Was I destined to spend yet another day in Baltimore?

Frogs and Scorpions

While still in line, I called Delta on my cell phone to see about other arrangements. There was a seat on a later flight. Before I even got to the ticket counter, I was rebooked with a different itinerary. Checking through security was slow. Everyone was given a pat down. We boarded the plane and prepared for departure. A stewardess announced we were leaving. *Tick-tick-tick*. No movement. Twenty minutes passed, thirty minutes, forty minutes. Forty-five minutes past our departure time, the same large, dignified looking black man in a suit walked onto the plane followed by four other men with guns. They walked past me toward the back of the plane. I listened carefully for any kind of a disturbance but heard none. Soon, four white passengers, some would call "redneck types" were escorted off the plane by the four men with guns and the large black man. The pilot made an announcement, "To explain what just happened, the passengers that just deplaned had made some suspicious remarks. Err...or rather were acting suspiciously. Err...I mean they were making some of the passengers uncomfortable by their actions. Err... they were suspicious!! We called the FBI, and they've been taken off the plane to be checked out. We now must get their baggage off the plane before we leave."

Over the next twenty minutes, we watched the ground crew bring eight cow-sized duffle bags from the cargo area of the plane and stack them up by two police cars waiting on the tarmac.

Of all the countries I've been to, the airport security is the tightest in Saudi Arabia, its tighter than China, much tighter than former Soviet Union countries. Most of the time I've been to

Saudi Arabia, as you enter the country, every bag is pawed through and searched. One time the inspection officer opened the suit case, turned it over, and dumped all the contents out on the table (One better not have any pink, laundry-bled underwear), rummaged through, then shoved the pile of items and the suitcase off the end of the table onto the floor for me to gather up while he looked at the next man's suitcase.

It looks like our airport security is headed toward what is common in other third world countries. It appears the "brainless devils" (as the Nigerian called them in his email to me) who perpetrated this horrible act against America have already made significant progress toward reducing us to the same level as those who have never known the sweet, happy, relative carefree lifestyle of living in a democracy. I pity them.

We flew from Baltimore to Atlanta, then onto Salt Lake City. It was on one of the first flights allowed in the air for nearly a week. When deplaning in Atlanta, I was the fourth one off the plane. At the end of the jetway, as people were entering the corridor, they were stopping. When I got to the stopped group, they were just standing there staring down the long corridor. Atlanta is the busiest airport in the US. It is nearly half a mile from one end to the other of the six corridors where the gates are located. The corridor was absolutely bare. Not one person in sight in a place that is always busy and crowded with throngs of travelers. The first man out stopped and turned to the rest and asked in amazement, "Where are we? Are we in the right place? Are we in Atlanta?"